The Concise Handbook of
Cultural, Political,
and
Pop Culture Terms

A Few Hundred Words You Need to Know to Sound Ten Times Smarter

BLOG
TWITTER
Diaspora

GTMO (Gitmo) refers to Guantanamo Bay...

Patricia St.E. Darlington
Rolda L. Darlington

RESEARCH/EDITORIAL ASSISTANTS
MARVA ADAMS • PAMELA ESTEVEZ • SONYA M. BROWN

Kendall Hunt
publishing company

Cover image © 2012, Shutterstock, Inc.

www.kendallhunt.com
Send all inquiries to:
4050 Westmark Drive
Dubuque, IA 52004-1840

Copyright © 2012 by Kendall Hunt Publishing Company

ISBN 978-1-4652-0420-2

Printed in the United States of America
10 9 8 7 6 5 4 3 2 1

CONTENTS

TO REORDER YOUR UPS DIRECT THERMAL LABELS:

1. Access our supply ordering web site at **UPS.COM**®
   or contact UPS at 800-877-8652.

2. Please refer to label #0277400801 when ordering.

ACKNOWLEDGEMENTS

I would like to take this opportunity to extend my deepest gratitude to two people who over the course of the past year have literally offered me their vision in place of my own. Sincere thanks to Pamela Estevez and Sonya Brown who are identified as editorial/research assistants on this project but who have personally given of their time, energy, and love to make this project a success. I would also like to thank Rolda Darlington for agreeing to work on this project with me. Her effort and dedication have proven her brilliance as an academic.

PStED

I would like to acknowledge a few special people in my life. To my supportive parents, brothers, uncle, and friends, Matthew and Jacqueline—my own personal cheerleading squad—I give my sincere thanks.

RLD

PREFACE

There are perhaps numerous reference works in popular American culture that define terms related to culture, politics, and pop culture. The uniqueness of this body of work lies in an effort to cross-reference the terms that we recognize as occupying an overlapping sphere, where politics meets pop culture and culture forms the bridge between them. In this body of work, readers can expect to familiarize themselves with the lexicon that has become popular among those who engage in discourse that is characterized as culturally relevant, politically savvy, and grounded in American popular culture.

Great consideration was given to including or excluding certain terms based on the term's relevance in the current political environment in which this handbook was prepared. While no determination was made on the importance of one particular piece of legislation over another, the authors employed a certain level of discretion, based on current social/political relevance, in order to choose words that best fit their intention. For example, while the authors included definitions for pieces of legislation such as Citizens United and the Buffett Rule, and terms such as Super PAC and Obamacare, it was recognized that these pieces of legislation and terms may be particularly useful for readers who may use this source as a reference dealing with current politics. In other words, this volume is not intended to be exhaustive. Rather, it is designed to be universally useful, but nuanced.

The terms selected by the authors were chosen after extensive observation and analysis of outlets that are concerned with the dissemination of information dealing with culture and politics. While it would have been a nearly impossible task to chronicle every term that has been used on the news, on the Internet, or in periodicals in recent times, great care was taken to create a volume that would help both the novice and the professional. Whether a reader is just getting into the world of politics or a student of sociology is interested in self-empowerment in the classroom, this book will serve as a launch pad for those pursuits. Likewise, for the professional who is concerned with keeping up with the ever-changing vernacular of a dynamic and culturally diverse world, as well as the instructor who aims to prepare students for the cultural and political landscape awaiting them outside of the classroom doors, this resource will be helpful for all.

It must be stated that, as with every piece of reference material, a certain level of subjectivity should be expected in its creation. The authors of this book resolved to prepare this reference material in such a way that their personal sentiments and preconceived notions were not determinative of the words they offer to their readers.

INTRODUCTION

Ethnicity, ethnocentricity, Afrocentricity, assimilation, enculturation, globalization, third world, free trade, intercultural, intracultural, multicultural, ageism, WMDs, gitmo, birther, LGBT, social media, tweet, facebook©— all words that have now become commonplace in the classrooms, boardrooms, and workshops and conversations of Americans. From the college class on diversity to the weekly ubiquitous HR diversity workshops of corporate America, within casual conversations along the hallways, and even by the water coolers of today's workplace, these words are tossed around like paperclips and are as casually used as Post-it® notes.

Every meeting seems to introduce a rapidly expanding list of new fangled words that each of us is expected to memorize and use at least once or twice in conversations and in e-mails to show just how up-to-date we are with all the politically correct speech and new lingo of multiculturalism. Nine times out of ten we find ourselves holding our breath after an utterance hoping it came out just right. Well, allow yourself to breathe. This book provides an easy-to-use guide to a few hundred of the most common words that anyone in today's culturally diverse society should know and be able to use with ease. The material in the Handbook is comprehensive enough for use in the ivory towers of academe and general enough to provide ease of use and quick reference from the bustling halls of corporate America to the family dinner tables and corner coffee bars.

As Americans, we can boast of living in what is perhaps the most culturally diverse nation on the planet. This diversity is all encompassing in its reach and includes people of different races/ethnicities, languages, religions, ages, political affiliation, mental and physical challenges, sexual orientations, and genders. Each aspect of our diversity is associated with a commonly shared set of symbols that allow us to participate in the most fundamental human interactions—that is, verbal/nonverbal exchanges which we have labeled "communication." However, not all of these symbols which are commonly shared are commonly understood. Even within the pluralistic society which we hold so dear, there are groups, or entities, which share symbols that are not so commonly shared with the rest of society.

Researchers, such as Lustig and Koester, have offered numerous approaches to defining culture including: (1) enumerating its components—that is, the parts that make it whole and which may include knowledge, belief, art, customs, language, and other behaviors learned as members of a society; (2) concentrating on the social heredity of a people, which suggests that all foreigners to that society must learn its practices, ideas, and its experiences; (3) examining the beliefs, values, and norms that are present in a group and evaluating how they function in guiding problem-solving behaviors; and (4) examining how people express their behavior patterns in everyday conversations and interactions. This fourth approach is what is generally referred to as cultural communication. Here, culture is seen as coming from the symbols and meanings that are deeply felt, commonly understood, and widely accessible, all of which can be attributed to behaviors by those within particular groups. The fourth approach is one that is particularly noteworthy in creating this compilation of cultural, political, and pop cultural terms. It should be noted that while this edition boasts of its concise nature, the compilation is comprised of a multitude of the words and terms generally found in the typical American vocabulary. Finally, in justifying the title, the word *terms* is used to suggest that this compilation contains definitions of "words" and or "groups of words."

The book is unique in that it:

- is intended to be a comprehensive, but user-friendly, compilation of words and terms found in the typical American vocabulary

- is written in a readable format appropriate for both academic and nonacademic readers

- serves as an excellent resource for courses in Intercultural Communication, Political Science, Sociology, Cultural Anthropology, and Ethnic studies

- serves as an excellent resource for Human Resources departments

- serves as an excellent resource for anyone involved in communication with individuals from different cultural groups

- provides a source guide for readers/researchers interested in determining the source of the definitions

- provides multiple definitions and sources where available

- includes numerous Internet sources for ease of reference and additional research opportunities

- is available in downloadable e-book format

- includes a CD-ROM supplemental resource

PART 1

Cultural Terms

A

Accents Lustig and Koester (2003) refer to accents as distinguishable marks of pronunciation. Accents are closely related to dialects. Research studies repeatedly demonstrate that speakers' accents are used as a cue to form impressions of them. They are characteristic pronunciations that determine both the regional and social background of the speaker.

Reference

Lusting, M., & Koester, J. (2003). *Intercultural competence: Interpersonal communication across cultures* (4th ed.). Boston: Allyn and Bacon.

Accommodation Ting-Toomey and Chung (2005) refer to accommodation as the interaction strategies that combine both majority and co-culture views. In comparison (to assimilation), co-culture members who use the strategy of accommodation attempt to maintain their cultural identity even while they strive to establish relationships with members of the dominant culture (Gamble & Gamble, 2005). The accommodation goal means that the marginalized group manages to keep co-cultural identity while striving for positive relationships with the dominant group (Pearson et al., 2006). A fundamentalist Christian woman never cuts her hair, always wears long dresses, and never wears makeup, but respects the right for her co-workers to have their own religious beliefs without interference from her (p. 171).

References

Gamble, T., & Gamble, M. (2005). *Communication works* (8th ed.). Boston: Allyn and Bacon.

Pearson, J., Nelson, P., Titsworth, S., & Harter L. (2006). *Human communication* (2nd ed.). New York: McGraw-Hill.

Ting-Toomey, S., & Chung, L. (2005). *Understanding intercultural communication*. Los Angeles: Roxbury.

Did you know...

The system of democracy was introduced 2,500 years ago in Athens, Greece.
Fast Fact on Politics: http://didyouknow.org/fastfacts/politics/

Acculturation Inherent in acculturation is the idea that most people, as they are adapting, are also holding on to many of the values, customs, and communication patterns found in their primary culture. Acculturation refers to the process by which a person's culture is modified through direct contact with or exposure to another culture (say through the mass media) (DeVito, 1992). Jandt (2004) also defines acculturation as the process of an immigrant learning and adopting the norms and values of a new host culture. In that process, the immigrant loses part of one national identity and adopts a new national identity. Unlike a temporary visitor, the immigrant must find a new source of livelihood and build a new life. For example, when immigrants settle into the United States (the host country), their own culture becomes influenced by the host culture. Gradually, the values, ways of behaving, and beliefs of the host culture become more and more a part of the immigrants' culture.

References

Chen, G., & Starosta, W. (1998). *Foundations of intercultural communication*. Boston: Allyn and Bacon.

Devito, J. (1992). *The interpersonal communication book* (6th ed.). New York: HarperCollins.

Gudykunst, W.B., & Kim, Y.Y. (1992). *Reading on communicating with strangers*.

New York: McGraw-Hill.

Hoebel, E.A., & Frost, E.L. (1976). *Culture and social anthropology.* New York: McGraw-Hill.

Jandt, F. (2004). *An introduction to intercultural communication: Identities in a global community* (4th ed.). Thousand Oaks, CA: Sage.

Kim, Y.Y. (1988). *Communication and cross-cultural adaption: An integrative theory.* Avon, England: Multilingual Matter.

Samovar, L., & Porter, R. (2004). *Communication between cultures* (5th ed.). Belmont, CA: Wadsworth.

Ting-Toomey, S., & Chung, L. (2005). *Understanding intercultural communication.* Los Angeles: Roxbury.

Activity Orientation An activity orientation defines how the people of a culture view human actions and the expression of self through activities (Lustig & Koester, 2003). It describes how people locate themselves on the being–becoming–doing continuum. Activity orientation deals with people in culture "being" (passively accepting), "being-in-becoming" (transforming), or "doing" (initiating action) (Jandt, 2004).

References

Jandt, F. (2004). *An introduction to intercultural communication: Identities in a global community* (4th ed.). Thousand Oaks, CA: Sage.

Lusting, M., & Koester, J. (2003). *Intercultural competence: Interpersonal communication across cultures* (4th ed.). Boston: Allyn and Bacon.

Adaptability Communication adaptability refers to our ability to change our interaction behaviors and goals to meet specific needs of the situation (Ting-Toomey & Chung, 2005). It signals our mindful awareness of the other person's perspectives, interests, goals, and communication approach, plus our willingness to modify our own behaviors and goals to adapt to the interaction situation. By mindfully tracking what is going on in the intercultural situation, both parties may modify their verbal and nonverbal behavior to achieve a more synchronized communication process.

References

Dodd, C.H. (1998). *Dynamics of intercultural communication* (5th ed.). New York: McGraw-Hill.

Ting-Toomey, S., & Chung, L. (2005). *Understanding intercultural communication.* Los Angeles: Roxbury.

Adaptation Words such as *assimilation, adjustment, acculturation,* and even *coping* are used to describe how individuals respond to their experiences in other cultures (Lusting & Koester, 2003). Many of these terms refer to how people from one culture react to prolonged contact with those from another. Adaptation is therefore the process by which people establish and maintain relatively stable, helpful, and mutually shared relationships with others upon relocating to an unfamiliar cultural setting. Note that this definition suggest that when individuals adapt to another culture they must learn how to "fit" themselves into it.

Reference

Lusting, M., & Koester, J. (2003). *Intercultural competence: Interpersonal communication across cultures* (4th ed.). Boston: Allyn and Bacon.

Adjustment stress Smith and Barna (1983) describe adjustment stress as a term used to indicate bodily physical tension that signals a person's readiness to face the challenges of the new cultural environment (as cited in Chen & Starosta, 1998). Sojourners often experience a great amount of psychological pressure in the process of intercultural adjustment.

Reference

Chen, G., & Starosta, W. (1998). *Foundations of intercultural communication.* Boston: Allyn and Bacon.

African American This term refers to those individuals of African (sub-Saharan) descent residing in the United States. This group though also characterized as Blacks, does not include Blacks from the Caribbean islands. The term originated in approximately 1980 and replaced other terms such as Negroes, Coloreds, and Afro Americans—terms which were used until the 1970s.

References

Baugh, J. (1999). *Out of the mouths of slave.* Austin, TX: University of Texas Press.
Hall, L.E. (2005). *Dictionary of multicultural psychology: Issues, terms, and concepts.* Thousand Oaks, CA: Sage.

Afrocentric The term Afrocentric became popular in American lexicon in the 1960s and 1970s as a result of the racial crisis occurring in United States society. The term, however, has a much earlier genesis in the literature of the late 1800s and early 1900s. According to Grant and Ladsen-Billings (1997), it refers to "the interpretation or reinterpretation of reality from perspectives that maintain and perpetuate African life and culture."

Reference

Grant, C.A., & Ladsen-Billings, G. (1997). *Dictionary of multicultural education.* Phoenix, AZ: Oryx.

Afrocentricity An orientation toward African or African American cultural standards, including beliefs and values, as the criteria for interpreting behaviors and attitudes. Involves interpreting history, culture, and behavior of Blacks worldwide in terms of dispersion or extension of African history and culture in the context of where it is found.

References

Jandt, F. (2007). *An introduction to intercultural communication: Identities in a global community* (5th ed.). Thousand Oaks, CA: Sage.
Martin, J.N., & Nakayama, T.K. (2007). *Intercultural communication in contexts* (4th ed.). New York: McGraw-Hill Companies, Inc.

Ageism This is the prejudice in favor of younger rather than older individuals, although in some cultures it is the other way around (Varner & Beamer, 1995).

Reference

Varner, I., & Beamer, L. (1995). *Intercultural communication: The global workplace.* Chicago: Irwin.

Alienation This causes a strong desire in sojourners to retain identification with their own culture (Chen & Starosta, 1998). The rejection of the host culture leads us to limit our social circle to acquaintances or work contacts and to seek out our own nationals for social enjoyment. Unable to employ the necessary skills for adjustment, we feel out of sync with the host culture and want desperately to return home.

Reference

Chen, G., & Starosta, W. (1998). *Foundations of intercultural communication.* Boston: Allyn and Bacon.

Amerasians Buck first used this term to describe the progeny of intergroup couples. The term was later applied to the offspring of Japanese "war brides" and U.S. military personnel from World War II. Today, the term is applied to the offspring of Asians and Americans.

References

Buck, P. (1930). *East wind, west wind.* New York: John Day.
Hall, L.E. (2005). *Dictionary of multicultural psychology: Issues, terms, and concepts.* Thousand Oaks, CA: Sage.

Did you know...

Victoria Woodhull (1838–1927) was the first woman to run for the presidency of the United States.
Fast Fact on Politics: http://didyouknow.org/fastfacts/politics/

American Indian According to Pavar, a person is recognized as American Indian only if that person has more than half Indian blood and the Indian community recognizes him or her as Indian. More generally however, the Bureau of Indian Affairs claims that an American Indian is one who is registered with or is an enrolled member of a tribe.

References

Bureau of Indian Affairs. (1998). *American Indians today.* Washington, DC: Author.
Pavar, S.L. (1992). *The rights of Indians and tribes: The ACLU guide to Indian and tribal rights.* Carbondale: Southern Illinois Press.

Anglocentrism Using Anglo or White cultural standards as the criteria for interpretations and judgments of behaviors and attitudes.

Reference

Martin, J.N., & Nakayama, T.K. (2007). *Intercultural communication in contexts* (4th ed.). New York: McGraw-Hill Companies, Inc.

Apartheid A policy which constitutes a set of racially restrictive laws. This policy originated in 1948 in South Africa. The system of Apartheid was dismantled between 1990 and 1994. Under this system everyone was required to register in one of four "racial" categories: Black, White, Indian, or Colored. These codes were used to determine where South Africans were allowed to live, their employment, access to public facilities, and other aspects of public life.

Reference

Martin, J.N., & Nakayama, T.K. (2007). *Intercultural communication in contexts* (4th ed.). New York: McGraw-Hill Companies, Inc.

Ascription The process by which others attribute identities to an individual.

Reference

Martin, J.N., & Nakayama, T.K. (2007). *Intercultural communication in contexts* (4th ed.). New York: McGraw-Hill Companies, Inc.

Arab American The community defined as Arab Americans can trace their roots to every Arab country. The majority of Arab Americans have ancestral ties to Lebanon, Syria, Palestine, Egypt, and Iraq. However, contrary to popular assumptions or stereotypes, the majority of Arab Americans are native born, and nearly 82% are U.S. citizens.

Reference

Arab American Institute. http://www.aaiusa.org/pages/arab-americans/

Asian American According to Magazine Publishers of America, Asian Americans are: "people who belong to at least one of fifteen distinct ethnic groups and national origins, including Bangladesh, Cambodian, Chinese, Filipino, Indian, Indonesian, Japanese, Korean, Laotians, Malaysian, Pakistanis, Sri Lankan, Taiwanese, Thai and Vietnamese."

Reference

Magazine Publishers of America. http://www.magazine.org/content/files/market_profile_asian.pdf

Assimilation This refers to the taking on the new culture's beliefs, values, and norms. It results from giving up one's original cultural identity and moving into full participation in the new culture (Jandt, 2004). The person identifies with the country and not an ethnic group. Assimilation is a long-term and sometimes multigenerational process. It is also known as attempting to "fit in," or join with, members of the dominant culture (Gamble & Gamble, 2005). They give up their own ways in an effort to assume the modes of behavior of the dominant culture. Lusting and Koester (2003) state that assimilation occurs when it is deemed relatively unimportant to maintain one's original cultural identity but is important to establish and maintain relationships with other cultures.

References

Gamble, T., & Gamble, M. (2005). *Communication works* (8th ed.). Boston: Allyn and Bacon.

Jandt, F. (2004). *An introduction to intercultural communication: Identities in a global community* (4th ed.). Thousand Oaks, CA: Sage.

Lusting, M., & Koester, J. (2003). *Intercultural competence: Interpersonal communication across cultures* (4th ed.). Boston: Allyn and Bacon.

Pearson, J., Nelson, P., Titsworth, S., & Harter L. (2006). *Human communication* (2nd ed.). New York: McGraw-Hill.

Wood, J. (2006). *Communication mosaics: An introduction to the field of communication* (4th ed.). Belmont, CA: Thomson Wadsworth.

Assimilationism Employing such metaphors as "melting pot" and "color-blind society," assimilationist messages project a societal vision in which immigrants and indigenous ethnic minorities are mainstreamed into the normative culture and institutions (Samovar, Porter, & McDaniel, 2006). In this vision, the government is responsible for universally applying societal rules to all its citizens irrespective of skin color and religious creed. Immigrants and ethnic minorities, in turn, are expected to assimilate themselves socially and culturally, so as to become fully functional in the American society.

Reference

Samovar, L., Porter, R., & McDaniel, E. (2006). *Intercultural communication: A reader* (11th ed.). Belmont, CA: Thomson Wadsworth.

Asylee A person living outside the country of nationality who is unable or unwilling to return because of actual persecution or a well-founded fear of persecution; the only difference between an asylee and a refugee is that an asylee is applying for admission in the country he or she is already in, whereas a refugee is applying for admission from outside the country he or she desires to enter.

Reference

Jandt, F. (2007). *An introduction to intercultural communication: Identities in a global community* (5th ed.). Thousand Oaks, CA: Sage.

Avowal The process by which an individual portrays himself or herself.

Reference

Martin, J.N., & Nakayama, T.K. (2007). *Intercultural communication in contexts* (4th ed.). New York: McGraw-Hill Companies, Inc.

Did you know...

Thomas Jefferson was the first president to be inaugurated in Washington, D.C. He was also the only president to walk to and from his inauguration.

Fast Fact on Politics: http://didyouknow.org/fastfacts/politics/

β

Bicultural The term bicultural is often used interchangeably with the term biracial. However, more specifically, it refers to the blending of two distinct cultures with the experience of living in a country other than one's native culture.

Reference

Merriam Webster Collegiate Dictionary. (1993). Springfield, MA: Merriam-Webster.

Bidialecticism Hall states that bidialecticism is a phenomenon noticed when individuals are capable of communicating in two dialects. The individual makes a decision to use the dialect appropriate to the situation. For example, an African American in a professional setting will choose to speak in Standard English, but may switch to Black English when conversing with another African American in an informal setting. This switch serves the purpose of establishing camaraderie. The switch may also be used to demonstrate empathy and understanding in situations where it is necessary to establish a comfort level with certain individuals.

Reference

Hall, L.E. (2005). *Dictionary of multicultural psychology: Issues, terms, and concepts.* Thousand Oaks, CA: Sage.

Biracial The term biracial is generally used to refer to individuals who share one Black parent and one White parent. This, however, is a misnomer as biracial individuals can have parents of any of the multitude of ethnicities that exist within our society. For example, a biracial child could have a parent who is Asian and a parent who is Black or a parent who is Native American and a parent who is White. The term biracial simply refers to any combination of heritages.

Reference

Online Merriam-Webster Dictionary. http://www.merriam-webster.com/dictionary/biracial?show=0&t=1342623658

Black English (see **Ebonics**) A nonstandard variety of English spoken by some African Americans. Also called "Black English Vernacular" or BEV.

Reference

> Online Merriam-Webster Dictionary. http://www.merriam-webster.com/dictionary/black+english

Blended identity The identity that occurs when individuals conform to the melting pot metaphor and racial/ethnic differences are removed from this particular collective identity.

Reference

> Orbe, M.P., & Harris, T.M. (2001). *Interracial communication: Theory into practice.* Belmont, CA: Wadsworth.

Did you know...

William Henry Harrison had the shortest term of office as U.S. president. He served for only thirty-two days, from March 4 to April 4, 1841.
Fast Fact on Politics: http://didyouknow.org/fastfacts/politics/

C

Camouflaged racism Involves distinctly racist behavior that bursts into public view from individuals whose racist outlooks and behavior generally remain hidden behind public statements and actions favoring racial equality. Majority-group members' racism breaks out of its camouflaged cover only when a race-related threat materializes, revealing in essence, their true colors.

Reference

> Doob, C.B. (2005). *Race, ethnicity, and the American urban mainstream.* Boston: Allyn and Bacon.

Caucasians This term originated in 1795 in the work of Johann Riedrich Blumembach. The term Caucasian has been used to describe most natives of Europe, West Asia, and North Africa and extends to the subcontinents of India. The word White is sometimes used synonymously with Caucasian.

Reference

Blumembach, J. (1865 [1795]). (T. Bendysh, trans.). *On the variety of mankind* (3rd ed.). London: Anthropological Society of London.

Chicano/Chicana The terms Chicano/Chicana have been used to describe Americans of Mexican descent. The term gained wide political and popular favor among Mexican American activists during the 1960s civil rights movement and has emerged as a political term, especially among academics and political activists. The term, however, can be used as a means of denigrating and stigmatizing one's social status.

Reference

Hall, L.E. (2005). *Dictionary of multicultural psychology: Issues, terms, and concepts.* Thousand Oaks, CA: Sage.

Chinese Americans Although approximately 90% of Chinese Americans are foreign born, the term is often used to refer to both, citizens and noncitizens. Until 1943, the law prevented Chinese immigrants from becoming American citizens. This law was later changed and people who had spent most of their lives in the United States became Chinese Americans.

Reference

Hall, L.E. (2005). *Dictionary of multicultural psychology: Issues, terms, and concepts.* Thousand Oaks, CA: Sage.

Chronemics The concept of time and the rules that govern its use. There are many variations among cultures and how they view time. The two primary distinctions are monochromic, which views time as linear and can be gained or lost and polychromic which sees time as circular and more holistic.

Reference

Martin, J.N., & Nakayama, T.K. (2007). *Intercultural communication in contexts* (4th ed.). New York: McGraw-Hill Companies, Inc.

Classism This is a practice where middle- and upper-class persons perpetuate discriminatory behaviors toward those of lower-class standing. Classism promotes the idea of separation; conscious efforts of "affluent" groups to do whatever they can do to avoid contact with the "less fortunate." As a result, stereotyping amongst lower-, middle-, and upper-class groups persist.

Reference

Orbe, M.P., & Harris, T.M. (2001). *Interracial communication: Theory into practice.* Belmont, CA: Wadsworth.

Did you know...

Fourteen of the forty-five vice presidents have become president. However, only five vice presidents have been elected to the presidency: John Adams, Thomas Jefferson, Martin Van Buren, Richard Nixon, and George Herbert Walker Bush.
Fast Fact on Politics: http://didyouknow.org/fastfacts/politics/

Co-culture The term co-culture was coined to describe groups of people who hold dual membership in the dominant culture and in a second one. Orbe (1998) states that co-culture is suggested to convey that no one culture is inherently superior to other coexisting cultures (Jandt, 2004). Yet, Samovar, Porter, and Stefani (1998) define co-culture as "a group whose beliefs or behaviors distinguish it from the larger culture of which it is a part and with which it shares numerous similarities" (Pearson et al., 2006). Samovar and Porter (1994) state that co-cultures are groups of people who live within a dominant culture, yet also are members of another culture that is not dominant in a particular society (Wood, 1997). For many years, social groups that lived in a dominant culture yet simultaneously belonged to a second culture were called subcultures. However, the prefix *sub-* connotes inferiority as if subcultures are somehow less complete than "regular" cultures.

References

Jandt, F. (2004). *An introduction to intercultural communication: Identities in a global community* (4th ed.). Thousand Oaks, CA: Sage.

Pearson, J., Nelson, P., Titsworth, S., & Harter L. (2006). *Human communication* (2nd ed.). New York: McGraw-Hill.

Samovar, L., Porter, R., & McDaniel, E. (2006). *Intercultural communication: A reader* (11th ed.). Belmont, CA: Thomson Wadsworth.

Wood, J. (1997). *Communication in our lives.* Belmont, CA: Wadsworth.

Code switching A technical term in communication that refers to the phenomenon of changing languages, dialects, or even accents. Code switching can also be defined in more basic terms as the process through which two or more individuals change from speaking one language to another during a conversation. People code switch for reasons such as wanting to accommodate the other speakers, to avoid accommodating others, and to express another aspect of their cultural identity.

Reference

Lusting, M., & Koester, J. (2006). *Intercultural competence: Interpersonal communication across cultures* (5th ed.). Boston: Allyn and Bacon.

Code systems These systems are the nonverbal actions that can communicate messages about our culture and ourselves. According to Lustig and Koester (2006), there are four types of code systems: chemical, dermal, physical, and artifactual.

Chemical—Chemical codes are based from chemically based body functions. Chemical codes include natural body odor, tears, sweat, gas, household smells, and similar phenomena. An individual's chemical system is distinct to their way of living, food preferences, habits, and environment. Such differences are often used to make judgments or interpretations about members of a culture.

Dermal—Dermal codes refer to the short-term changes in skin texture or sensitivity that result from physical or psychological reactions to the environment. Dermal codes include blushing, blanching, goose flesh, and related experiences. High-context cultures may use dermal codes as clues to how to interact with people from other cultures.

Physical—The physical code system refers to the relatively unchanging aspects of the body such as weight, body shape, facial features, skin color, eye color, hair, characteristics that denote age and gender, and similar features.

Artifactual—Artifactual codes consist of creations that people make, use, or wear. These aspects of material culture include the tools, clothing, buildings, furnishings, jewelry, lighting, and color schemes that are common to the members of a culture.

Reference

Lusting, M., & Koester, J. (2006). *Intercultural competence: Interpersonal communication across cultures* (5th ed.). Boston: Allyn and Bacon.

Collectivism The tendency to focus on the goals, needs, and views of the in-group rather than the individuals' own goals, needs, and views.

Reference

> Martin, J.N., & Nakayama, T.K. (2007). *Intercultural communication in contexts* (4th ed.). New York: McGraw-Hill Companies, Inc.

Colonialism The policy or practice of acquiring full or partial political control over another country, occupying it with settlers, and exploiting it economically. Three of the most notable colonizers were Britain, France, and Spain.

Reference

> Martin, J.N., & Nakayama, T.K. (2007). *Intercultural communication in contexts* (4th ed.). New York: McGraw-Hill Companies, Inc.

Color-blind racism An ideological position asserting Whites' frequently proclaimed desire to live in a society in which race no longer matters. Many White Americans argue that the United States is a largely discrimination-free society in which racism is minimal and declining in significance.

Reference

> Dood, C.B. (2005). *Race, ethnicity, and the American urban mainstream*. Boston: Allyn and Bacon.

Communication apprehension Fear or anxiety associated with either real or anticipated communication with another person or persons. It is the uncertainty about communication, usually resulting in withdrawal, shyness, reticence, or high anxiety about communication with another person, in a group, in a meeting, or in a public setting. Research suggests that U.S. society stresses verbal performance so much that U.S. speakers may experience more pressure than those from other cultures.

Reference

> Dodd, C.H. (1998). *Dynamics of intercultural communication* (5th ed.). Boston: McGraw Hill.

Community In intercultural terms, community refers to a group of individuals who have learned how to communicate honestly with each other. Peck articulates several aspects of "true community" that contribute to maximizing the potential for interracial communication interactions.

Inclusiveness—Refers to a general acceptance and appreciation of differences, not as necessarily positive or negative but just as different.

Commitment—Involves a strong willingness to coexist and work through barriers that hinder community development. Part of this commitment to community is a faithfulness to work through both the positive and negative experiences associated with the tensions of racial interactions (a.k.a. "Hanging in there when the going gets rough.").

Consensus—Acknowledging and processing cultural differences. Working through differences in opinions and seek a general agreement or accord among members.

Contemplation—Being aware of the multicultural environment that exists. Individuals must be willing to discard their "masks of composure" and expose their inner selves to others, thus assuming a certain degree of vulnerability.

Graceful fighting—Agreements and disagreements should be articulated, negotiated, and possibly resolved, productively.

Reference

Peck, S. (1987). *The different drum: Community-making and peace.* New York: Simon & Schuster.

Did you know...

Ronald Reagan was the U.S. presidential candidate with the highest popular vote ever. In 1984 he received 54,455,075 votes. He was also the candidate with the highest electoral vote: 525, in 1984.
Fast Fact on Politics: http://didyouknow.org/fastfacts/politics/

Context This refers to the environment in which the communication process takes place. It is the information that surrounds an event and it is inextricably bound up with the meaning of that event (Martin, Nakayama, & Flores, 2002). The events that combine to produce a given meaning are in different proportions depending on the culture. The cultures of the world can be compared on a scale from high to low context.

Reference

Martin, J.N., Nakayama, T.K., & Flores, L.A. (2002). *Readings in intercultural communication: Experiences and contexts.* New York : McGraw-Hill

Creoles There are several definitions associated with the term Creole. One of them relates to Creole as a vernacular language that developed in colonial European plantation settlements in the 17th and 18th centuries as a result of contact between groups that spoke mutually unintelligible languages. Most commonly, creoles have resulted from the interactions between speakers of nonstandard varieties of European languages and speakers of non-European languages.

A second definition relates to Creole as a cultural reference. The term Creole was coined in the 16th century to refer to locally born individuals of Spanish, Portuguese, or African descent as distinguished from those born in Spain, Portugal, or Africa. By the early 17th century, the word was adopted into French (and, to some extent, English) usage to refer to people of African or European descent who had been born in the American and Indian Ocean colonies.

References

Creole languages. (2012). In *Encyclopædia Britannica.* http://www.britannica.com/EBchecked/topic/142562/creole-languages

Martin, J.N., & Nakayama, T.K. (2007). *Intercultural communication in contexts* (4th ed.). New York: McGraw-Hill Companies, Inc.

Cuban Americans This term refers to U.S. citizens who trace their origin to Cuba. The Cuban American community is well assimilated in the United States. Moreover, because of its size, this group has significant political influence. Many Cubans migrated to the United States when fleeing Castro's regime in search of political asylum. Cuban Americans form the third largest Hispanic group in the United States and also the largest group of Hispanics of European ancestry, predominantly Spanish descent.

Reference

Pew Hispanic Center. (2009). Detailed Hispanic origin: 2007. http://www. pewhispanic.org/2009/03/05/statistical-portrait-of-hispanics-in-the-united-states-2007/2007-portrait-of-hispanics-05/

Cultural adaptation (see **Acculturation**) Cultural adaptation refers to the process that people who belong to a different culture must experience to adapt to a new environment. Martin and Nakayama (2007) offer three models of cultural adaptation: the AUM model, the transition model, and the integrated theory of communication and cultural adaptation model.

References

Hall, L.E. (2005). *Dictionary of multicultural psychology: Issues, terms, and concepts.* Thousand Oaks, CA: Sage.

Martin, J.N., & Nakayama, T.K. (2007). *Intercultural communication in contexts* (4th ed.). New York: McGraw-Hill Companies, Inc.

Cultural adjustment This term describes the process of going through transitions and adapting to the stresses of a new culture (Dodd, 1998).

Reference

Dodd, C.H. (1998). *Dynamics of intercultural communication* (5th ed.). Boston: McGraw-Hill.

Cultural borders Cultural borders are generally socially constructed. These borders can be formed around religious, economic, political, and even ethnic identities. Conflict can emerge when "outsiders" attempt to cross cultural boundary lines without the invitation of the in-group.

Reference

Erickson, F. (1997). Culture in society and in educational practices. In J.A. Banks & C.A.M. Banks (Eds.), *Multicultural education: Issues and perspectives.* Needham Heights, MA: Allyn and Bacon.

Cultural competence This state is achieved when individuals have the ability both to adapt their messages specifically for others and are able to obtain immediate interpretation. Samovar and Porter (1997) also suggest that cultural competence is the demonstrated ability to enact a cultural identity in a mutually appropriate and effective manner. Cultural competence should be recognized as distinct from intercultural competence which, according to Lustig and Koester (2003), requires attention to and appreciation of several variables including motivation for communication, context, appropriateness, effectiveness, knowledge, and actions. Furthermore, Samovar and Porter (1997) suggest that intercultural competence is the reinforcement of culturally different identities that are salient in the particular situation.

References

Lustig, M.W., & Koester, J. *Intercultural competence: Interpersonal communication across cultures.* Boston: Allyn and Bacon, Pearson Publication.

Samovar, L.A., & Porter, R.E. *Intercultural communication: A reader.* London, UK: Wadsworth Publishing Company.

Did you know...

Technically, John Hanson was the first president of the United States. Although George Washington was the first president under the U.S. Constitution of 1789, the United States was an independent nation for thirteen years before the Constitution was signed. For one year during this time, John Hanson served as "President of the United States in Congress assembled."
Fast Fact on Politics: http://didyouknow.org/fastfacts/politics/

Cultural context The beliefs, values, attitudes, meaning, social hierarchies, religion, notions of time, and roles of a group of people that help participants form and interpret messages (Verderber & Verderber, 2005).

Reference

Verderber, R., & Verderber, K. (2005). *Communicate!* (11th ed.). Belmont, CA: Wadsworth.

Cultural diversity According to O'Hare (1997), with the face of the nation changing, the culture of the Founding Fathers—White, male, Christian, and English-speaking—is less widely accepted as the standard of normality than it was in the past. Members of this co-culture are already a minority, and although many aspects of their culture remain dominant, members of other co-cultures are asserting the equal worth of their cultural characteristics. Females, people of color, homosexuals, the elderly, people with physical and mental challenges, non-Christians, and other groups that have long been oppressed are refusing to accept second-class status. To communicate effectively, everyone must recognize the heterogeneity of our society (i.e., members of both sexes and all ethnic, racial, and religious groups; people of all ages and abilities) must view each other without prejudice and with respect for the value of cultures other than their own. This heterogeneity forms the foundation of cultural diversity.

Reference

O'Hair, D., Friedrich, G., Wiemann, J., & Wiemann, M. (1997). *Competent communication* (2nd ed.). New York: St. Martin's.

Cultural hegemony This refers to the idea that any one culture can dominate another culture. In this process, it is believed that what is being transmitted are the values of the culture. The receiving culture can unconsciously, or perhaps uncritically, absorb the values.

Reference

Jandt, F. (2007). *An introduction to intercultural communication: Identities in a global community* (5th ed.). Thousand Oaks, CA: Sage.

Cultural identity This term refers to ones' sense of belonging to a particular culture or ethnic group (Lustig & Koester, 2003). It is formed in a process that results from membership in a particular culture, and it involves learning about and accepting the traditions, heritage, language, religion, ancestry, aesthetics, thinking patters, and social structures of a culture. That is, people internalize the beliefs, values, and norms of their culture and identify with the culture as part of their self-concept.

Reference

Lusting, M., & Koester, J. (2003). *Intercultural competence: Interpersonal communication across cultures* (4th ed.). Boston: Allyn and Bacon.

Cultural noise Results from preconceived, unyielding attitudes derived from a group or society about how members of that culture should act or in what they should or shouldn't believe (Berko, Wolvin, & Wolvin, 2004).

Reference

Berko, R., Wolvin, A., & Wolvin, D. (2004). *Communicating: A social and career focus* (9th ed.). Boston: Houghton Mifflin.

Cultural patterns This refers to the way cultures orient themselves to activities, social relations, the self, the world, and time (Lusting & Koester, 2003). According to a theory developed by F. R. Kluckhohn and F.L. Strodtbeck in 1961, cultural patterns are described as "value orientations" (Samovar & Porter, 2004). Kluckhon and Strodtbeck also believe that **value orientations** are the means society uses to solve the universal problems of daily life (Chen & Starosta, 1998). These **orientations** or **pattern**s tell the members of the culture what is important and also offer guidance for living their life.

References

Chen, G., & Starosta, W. (1998). *Foundations of intercultural communication.* Boston: Allyn and Bacon.

Lusting, M., & Koester, J. (2003). *Intercultural competence: Interpersonal communication across cultures* (4th ed.). Boston: Allyn and Bacon.

Samovar, L., & Porter, R. (2004). *Communications between cultures* (5th ed.). Belmont, CA: Wadsworth

Cultural pluralism According to *Merriam-Webster's Dictionary*, pluralism is a state of society in which members of diverse ethnic, racial, religious, or social groups maintain an autonomous participation in and development of their traditional culture or special interest within the confines of a common civilization. The term cultural pluralism describes the diversity of cultures coming together in a harmonious fashion without any particular culture dominating the social norms. In this case, each culture can maintain their uniqueness while combining to form a greater whole.

Reference

Merriam Webster Collegiate Dictionary. (1993). Springfield, MA: Merriam-Webster.

Culture Although the word culture is part of our everyday vocabulary, it is difficult to define. There are numerous meanings of this term. Culture can be a set of fundamental ideas, practices, and experiences of a group of people that are symbolically transmitted generation to generation through a learning process (Chen & Starsota, 1998). Culture may also refer to beliefs, norms, and attitudes that are used to guide our behaviors and to solve human problems. Culture can be further defined as a negotiated set of shared symbolic systems that guide individuals' behaviors and incline them to function as a group. The term culture originates from the Latin word *cultura* or *cultus* as in "*agri culture*, the cultivation of soil. From its root meaning of an activity, culture became transformed into a condition, a state of being cultivated" (Freilich, 1989, as cited in Ting-Toomey 1999). Cooper, Calloway-Thomas, and Simonds (2007) go further to define culture not only as a set of values and beliefs, but as norms and customs, and rules and codes that socially define a group of people, bind them to one another, and give a sense of commonality. Jandt (2004) defines culture as a community or population sufficiently large enough to be self-sustaining, being able to produce new generation of members without relying on outsiders. In this sense, culture is a process of social transmission of thoughts and behaviors learned from birth in the family and schools over the course of generations. Culture is the coherent, learned, shared view that a group of people has about life's concerns that ranks what is important, instills attitudes about what things are appropriate, and prescribes behavior, given that some things have more significance than others (Varner & Beamer, 1995). Culture is a communication phenomenon because it is passed from generation to generation through interactions. Knapp and Hall (2006) believe that we are learning about culture when we learn the rules and/or norms people expect or behavior to match. All of us exist within several cultures—our family, our religious group, our social class, our age group, our school, the place we work, our gender, and our society (Knapp & Hall, 2006). Culture guides behavior and communication. It tells you who you are, how to act, how to think, how to talk, and how to listen (Gamble & Gamble, 2005). Wood (2011) states that "culture is one of the most important systems within which communication occurs" (p. 145). Communication is closely linked to culture, because communication expresses, sustains, and alters cultures. Your culture directly shapes how you communicate, teaching you whether interrupting is appropriate, how much eye contact is polite, and whether argument and conflict are desirable in groups and personal relationships.

References

Berko, R., Wolvin, A., & Wolvin, D. (2004). *Communicating: A social and career focus* (9th ed.). Boston: Houghton Mifflin.

Chen, G., & Starosta, W. (1998). *Foundations of intercultural communication.* Boston: Allyn and Bacon.

Cooper, P., Calloway-Thomas, C., & Simonds, C. (2007). *Intercultural communication: A text with readings.* Boston: Pearson, Allyn and Bacon.

Devito, J. (2002). *Essentials of human communication* (4th ed.). Boston: Allyn and Bacon.

Gamble, T., & Gamble, M. (2005). *Communication works* (8th ed.). Boston: Allyn and Bacon.

Goodall, Jr., H.L., & Goodall, S. (2006). *Communicating in professional contexts: Skills, ethics, and technologies* (2nd ed.). Belmont, CA: Thomson Wadsworth.

Jandt, F. (2004). *An introduction to intercultural communication: Identities in a global community* (4th ed.). Thousand Oaks, CA: Sage.

Knapp, M., & Hall, J. (2006). *Nonverbal communication in human interaction* (6th ed.). Belmont, CA: Thomson Wadsworth.

Moon, D.G. (1996). Concepts of culture: Implications for intercultural communication research. *Communications Quarterly, 44,* 70–84.

Pearson, J., Nelson, P., Titsworth, S., & Harter L. (2006). *Human communication* (2nd ed.). New York: McGraw-Hill.

Ting-Toomey, S. (1999). *Communicating across cultures.* New York: Guilford Press.

Ting-Toomey, S., & Chung, L. (2005). *Understanding intercultural communication.* Los Angeles: Roxbury.

Samovar, L., Porter, R., & McDaniel, E. (2006). *Intercultural communication: A reader* (11th ed.). Belmont, CA: Thomson Wadsworth.

Varner, I., & Beamer, L. (1995). *Intercultural communication: The global workplace.* Chicago: Irwin.

Weaver, G.R. (2000). *Culture, communication, and conflict: Readings in intercultural relations* (2nd ed.). Boston:Pearson

Wood, J. T. (2011). *Communication in our lives* (6th ed.). Boston, MA:Wadsworth.

Did you know...

Coffee is the second largest item of international commerce in the world. The largest is petrol.

Human World: http://home.bitworks.co.nz/trivia/human.htm

Culture and uncertainty avoidance Uncertainty avoidance refers to the degree to which people in a country prefer to structured over unstructured situations: from relatively flexible to extremely rigid (Jandt, 2004). It also refers to the extent to which members of a culture do not mind conflicts or uncertain situations and the extent to which they try to avoid those uncertain situations. In these cultures, such situations are avoided by maintaining strict codes of behavior and a belief in absolute truths. People from different cultures differ greatly in their attitudes toward uncertainty and how to deal with it, attitudes that affect perceptual accuracy (Devito, 2002). In some cultures, people do little to avoid uncertainty and have little anxiety about not knowing what will happen next. Uncertainty to them is a normal part of life and is accepted as it comes. Obviously, some cultures have a high need for information and certainty (Dodd, 1998). For them, avoiding uncertainty would be very difficult without increasing the number of rules of behavior to compensate for the uncertainty. Other cultures, however, seem more comfortable dealing with diversity and ambiguity. As a characteristic of culture, uncertainty avoidance indicates the extent to which people within a culture are made anxious by situations that they perceive as unstructured, unclear, or unpredictable (Klopf & McCroskey, 2007).

Members of high uncertainty avoidance cultures always try to reduce the level of ambiguity and uncertainty in social and organizational life. They pursue job and life security, avoid risk taking, resist changes, fear failure, and seek behavioral rules that can be followed in interactions. Strong or high uncertainty avoidance cultures prefer clear procedures and conflict-avoidance behaviors (Ting-Toomey & Chung, 2005). These types of cultures are active, aggressive, emotional, compulsive, security seeking, and intolerant.

Members of low uncertainty avoidance cultures tend to better tolerate the deviant behaviors and unusual stress connected with the uncertainty and ambiguity. As a result, they take more initiative, show greater flexibility, and feel more relaxed in interactions. Weak or low uncertainty avoidance cultures encourage risk taking and conflict-approaching modes (Ting-Toomey & Chung, 2005). They are contemplative, less aggressive, unemotional, relaxed, accepting personal risks, and relatively tolerant. Uncertainty-accepting cultures tolerate ambiguity, uncertainty, and diversity. They are less likely to have a rule for everything and more likely to tolerate general principles (Dodd, 1998). Uncertainty-rejecting cultures have difficulty with ambiguity, uncertainty, and diversity. These cultures are more likely to have lots of rules; more likely to want to know exactly how to behave; and more likely to reject outsiders such as immigrants, refugees, and migrants who look and act different from them.

References

Adler, R., & Rodman, G. (2006). *Understanding human communication* (9th ed.). New York: Oxford University Press.

Chen, G., & Starosta, W. (1998). *Foundations of intercultural communication.* Boston: Allyn and Bacon.

Devito, J. (1992). *The interpersonal communication book* (6th ed.). New York: HarperCollins.

Devito, J. (2002). *Essentials of human communication* (4th ed.). Boston: Allyn and Bacon.

Dodd, C.H. (1998). *Dynamics of intercultural communication* (5th ed.). Boston: McGraw-Hill.

Hofstede, G. (1997). *Cultures and organizations: Software of the mind.* New York: McGraw-Hill.

Jandt, F. (2004). *An introduction to intercultural communication: Identities in a global community* (4th ed.). Thousand Oaks, CA: Sage.

Klopf, D.W., & McCroskey, J.C. (2007). *Intercultural communication encounters.* Boston: Allyn and Bacon.

Ting-Toomey, S., & Chung, L. (2005). *Understanding intercultural communication.* Los Angeles: Roxbury.

Culture shock (see **U-curve model)** A relatively short-term feeling of disorientation and discomfort due to the unfamiliarity of surroundings and the lack of familiar cues in the environment.

References

Colman, A.M. (2001). Culture shock. In *Dictionary of psychology.* New York: Oxford University Press.

McMillan, J.H. (1996). Culture shock. In *Concise encyclopedia of psychology.* New York: Oxford University Press.

Discrimination Allport (1954) defines discrimination as any behavior that denies individuals or groups of people the equality of treatment they may wish. Discrimination is the act of sifting out and selecting according to bias toward something or someone (Varner & Beamer, 1995). Discrimination often occurs in the areas of employment, residential housing, political rights, educational and recreational opportunities, and other social privileges. Discrimination refers to the verbal and nonverbal actions that carry out prejudiced attitudes (Ting-Tommey & Chung, 2005). According to Feagin (1989), four basic types of discriminatory practices exist in a society: isolate discrimination, small group discrimination, direct institutional discrimination, and indirect institutional discrimination. When an in-group member engages in isolate discrimination, harmful verbal and nonverbal action is intentionally targeted toward an out-group member. This discriminatory behavior occurs on an individual basis. It ranges from the use of racist slurs to violent physical action. If there is a community-prescribed endorsement of discrimination, we can call this direct institutional discrimination. Such practices are not isolated incidents but are carried out routinely by a large-scale number of individuals protected by the laws of a large-scale community. Indirect institutional discrimination is broad practice that indirectly affects group members without such intention.

References

Allport, G. (1954). *The nature of prejudice.* Cambridge, MA: Addison-Wesley

Chen, G., & Starosta, W. (1998). *Foundations of intercultural communication.* Boston: Allyn and Bacon.

Feagin, J.R. (1989). *Racial and ethnic relations* (3rd ed.). Englewood Cliffs, NJ: Prentice Hall.

Klopf, D.W., & McCroskey, J.C. (2007). *Intercultural communication encounters.* Boston: Allyn and Bacon.

O'Hair, D., Friedrich, G., Wiemann, J., & Wiemann, M. (1997). *Competent communication* (2nd ed.). New York: St. Martin's.

Ting-Toomey, S., & Chung, L. (2005). *Understanding intercultural communication.* Los Angeles: Roxbury.

Varner, I., & Beamer, L. (1995). *Intercultural communication: The global workplace.* Chicago: Irwin.

Discursive imperialism The labeling of a group as a dehumanized "other," which facilitates actions taken against it.

Reference

Jandt, F. (2007). *An introduction to intercultural communication: Identities in a global community* (5th ed.). Thousand Oaks, CA: Sage.

Duality This refers to one's ability to accommodate to both the original and the host culture while living in a new environment and our achievement of a sense of autonomy and bicultural independence. Such flexibility provides us with new skills to value cultural contrasts to integrate new and existing beliefs and rules. The attitudes of open-mindedness and flexibility are required in this situation to maintain an appropriate balance between continuity and growth.

Reference

Chen, G., & Starosta, W. (1998). *Foundations of intercultural communication.* Boston: Allyn and Bacon.

E

Ebonics (or Black English) Like all dialects, Ebonics (a combination of the words *ebony* and *phonics*) is not slang, sloppy speech, incorrect grammar, or broken English. Rather, it reflects an intersection of West African languages and European American English, which initially developed during the European slave trade and the enslavement of African peoples throughout the Americas and elsewhere. Ebonics, or Black English, shares a vocabulary with mainstream English but is governed by distinct grammatical usages and differences in pronunciation.

Reference

Lustig, M., & Koester, J. (2006). *Intercultural competence: Interpersonal communication across cultures* (5th ed.). Boston: Allyn and Bacon

Enculturation The term enculturation denotes the total activity of learning one's culture. More specifically, enculturation is, as Hoebel and Frost say, "conscious or unconscious conditioning occurring within that process whereby the individual, as child and adult, achieves competence in a particular culture" (Samovar, Porter, & McDaniel, 2006). From infancy, members of a culture learn their patterns of behavior and ways of thinking until most of them become internalized and habitual. Enculturation usually takes place through interaction, observation, and imitation.

References

Devito, J. (2007). *The interpersonal communication book* (11th ed.). Boston: Allyn and Bacon.

Hoebel, E.A., & Frost, E.L. (1976). *Culture and social anthropology*. New York: McGraw-Hill.

Samovar, L., Porter, R., & McDaniel, E. (2006). *Intercultural communication: A reader* (11th ed.). Belmont, CA: Thomson Wadsworth.

Ethnic agglomeration effect This term refers to the causal impact produced when increasing numbers of a given ethnic group settle in a city and create more jobs for the group's members. For example, between 1880 and 1920, New York received more immigrants than any other state. As a result, Jewish- and Italian-owned shops and small factories created job opportunities usually reserved for members of their respective groups.

Reference

Doob, C.B. (2005). *Race, ethnicity, and the American urban mainstream*. Boston: Allyn and Bacon.

Ethnic cleansing A process by which members of one ethnic group can systematically eliminate the members of another ethnic group, usually through violent means claiming the territory as their own. This process is generally employed as a means of "purifying" the dominant group. Examples of ethnic cleansing can be traced back to Yugoslavia and Rwanda in the 1990s and Darfur in the 2000s. Genocide is generally employed as a method of ethnic cleansing.

Reference

Danner, M. (1997). Ethnic cleansing in former Yugoslavia. *New York Review of Books*.

Ethnic enclaves Interconnected sets of small businesses belonging to a single ethnic group, located in its own neighborhood, and usually serving both the immediate ethnic community and the society at large.

Reference

Doob, C.B. (2005). *Race, ethnicity, and the American urban mainstream*. Boston: Allyn and Bacon.

Ethnic groups According to Banks (1984), Ethnic groups share a sense of heritage, history, and origin from an area outside of residence (Banks, 1984; Samovar, Porter, & McDaniel, 2006). Ethnic groups, in most but not all cases, share racial characteristics, and many have a specific history of having experienced discrimination. In the United States, ethnic group members include African Americans, Asian Americans (e.g., Japanese Americans, Chinese Americans, Vietnamese Americans, Korean Americans), Mexican Americans, Polish Americans, Irish Americans, Native American Indians, and Jewish Americans, just to name a few examples.

References

Banks, J. (1984). *Teaching Strategies for Ethnic Studies* (3rd ed.). Boston: Allyn and Bacon.

Dodd, C.H. (1998). *Dynamics of intercultural communication* (5th ed.). Boston: McGraw-Hill.

Jandt, F. (2004). *An introduction to intercultural communication: Identities in a global community* (4th ed.). Thousand Oaks, CA: Sage.

Samovar, L., Porter, R., & McDaniel, E. (2006). *Intercultural communication: A reader* (11th ed.). Belmont, CA: Thomson Wadsworth.

Ethnic identity According to Collier and Thomas (1988), ethnic identity refers to identification with and perceived acceptance into a group with shared heritage and culture (Jandt, 2004).

References

Collier, M.J., & Thomas, M. (1988). Cultural identity: An interpretive perspective. *International and Intercultural Communication Annual, 12*, 99–120.

Jandt, F. (2004). *An introduction to intercultural communication: Identities in a global community* (4th ed.). Thousand Oaks, CA: Sage.

Ethnic pluralism Describes ethnic groups' respective contributions to American society, stressing both their current distinctive qualities and their important functions. Unlike assimilation-oriented theories, ethnic pluralism perspectives do not contend that all groups will simply blend into the larger culture. Instead, they argue that various racial and ethnic groups will find it in their interest to retain some of their own cultural traditions and activities.

Reference

Doob, C.B. (2005). *Race, ethnicity, and the American urban mainstream*. Boston: Allyn and Bacon.

Ethnic succession The process by which the presence of established ethnic groups affect the economic opportunities of the groups arriving afterward. Members of a group move out of a job market or residential area only when it serves their purpose to do so.

Reference

Doob, C.B. (2005). *Race, ethnicity, and the American urban mainstream*. Boston: Allyn and Bacon.

Ethnicity This term relates to a group of people possessing a real or supposed ancestry, memories of a shared historical past, and concentration on symbolic elements representing their people such as kinship patterns, religious affiliation, language, nationality, physical contact, or any combination of these (Klopf & McCroskey, 2007). The concept does not imply prejudice, discrimination, oppression, or power, and is limited to homogeneous groups. Ethnicity is actually a term that is used to refer to a wide variety of groups who might share historical origins, nation-state, or cultural system (Lustig & Koester, 2003).

References

Lusting, M., & Koester, J. (2003). *Intercultural competence: Interpersonal communication across cultures* (4th ed.). Boston: Allyn and Bacon.
Klopf, D.W., & McCroskey, J.C. (2007). *Intercultural communication encounters*. Boston: Allyn and Bacon.

Ethnocentrism Ting-Toomey and Chung (2005) state that ethnocentrism comes from two Greek words and can be broken down into its components. Ethno refers to "one's own ethnic or cultural group," and centrism means that "one's own group should be looked upon as the center of the world." Ethnocentrism is the process of valuing your own ethnic culture so much that you are comfortable only with people similar to yourself (O'Hair et al., 1997). Jandt (2004) defines ethnocentrism as the negative judging of aspects of another culture by the standards of one's own culture. To be ethnocentric is to believe in the superiority of one's own culture. As a result, we expect that all other groups should follow our way of living and behaving. Ethnocentrism is a major roadblock toward competent communication because it prevents an individual or group from understanding the expectations and goals of culturally different people.

References

Chen, G., & Starosta, W. (1998). *Foundations of intercultural communication*. Boston: Allyn and Bacon.

Damen, L. (1987). *Cultural learning: The fifth dimension in the language classroom*. Reading, MA: Addison-Wesley.

Haviland, W.A. (2002). *Cultural anthropology*. Belmont, CA: Wadsworth.

Jandt, F. (2004). *An introduction to intercultural communication: Identities in a global community* (4th ed.). Thousand Oaks, CA: Sage.

Nanda, S., & Warms, R.L. (1998). *Cultural anthropology* (6th ed.). Belmont, CA: Wadsworth.

O'Hair, D., Friedrich, G., Wiemann, J., & Wiemann, M. (1997). *Competent communication* (2nd ed.). New York: St. Martin's.

Samovar, L., Porter, R., & McDaniel, E. (2006). *Intercultural communication: A reader* (11th ed.). Belmont, CA: Thomson Wadsworth.

Sumner, W. (1940). *Folkways*. Boston: Ginn.

Ting-Toomey, S., & Chung, L. (2005). *Understanding intercultural communication*. Los Angeles: Roxbury.

Varner, I., & Beamer, L. (1995). *Intercultural communication: The global workplace*. Chicago: Irwin.

Ethnomethodology This is a research method used to evaluate the behavior of people in real time. One way of doing this is by breaking the expected rules and norms of behaviors within certain established settings and observing the responses that are elicited from those being observed. Babbie (2007) provides an excellent example of this methodology at work. He suggests that the researcher enter a crowded elevator and face the back of the elevator rather than looking at the numbers go by, and observe the reaction of the other riders. These responses form real-time behaviors. He recommends repeating this pattern over several occasions in order to determine the particular responses of certain groups.

Reference

Babbie, E. (2007). *The practice of social research* (11th ed.). Belmont, CA: Wadsworth.

Ethos This Greek word means "character." Ethos is used to describe the guiding beliefs or ideals that characterize a community, nation, or ideology (Weiss & Taruskin, 1984). Ethos can simply mean the disposition, character, or fundamental values peculiar to a specific person, people, culture, or movement.

Reference

Weiss, P., & Taruskin, R. (1984). *Music in the western world: A history in documents.* Belmont, CA: Thomson/Schirmer.

Euro American The term refers to a U.S. citizen or resident of European descent. It was created to describe people who were of European and American descent.

Reference

The Ohio State University. (2012). Identity terms definitions. http://mcc.osu.edu/about-us/identity-terms-definitions/

Eurocentrism This is the practice of viewing the world from a European point of view. It is generally associated with the perspective that Europe provides a dominant position in the world thereby setting the standards of religious, social, racial, and cultural norms.

Reference

Amin, S. (1989). *Eurocentrism.* New York: Monthly Review Press.

Face According to Ting-Toomey (2005), the term face is "the interaction between the degree of threats or considerations one party offers to another party, and the degree of claim for a sense of self-respect put forth by the other party in a given situation." Rosenberg (2004) suggests that face is a multifaceted term, and its meaning is inextricably linked with culture and other terms such as honor and its opposite, humiliation. "Saving face" or "giving face" has different levels of importance, depending on the culture or society with which one is dealing.

References

Rosenberg, Sarah. (2004, February). Face. In G. Burgess and H. Burgess (Eds.), *Beyond intractability*. Conflict Information Consortium, University of Colorado, Boulder.

Ting-Toomey, S. (2005). The matrix of face: An updated face-negotiation theory. In W.B. Gudykunst (Ed.), *Theorizing about intercultural communication*. Thousand Oaks, CA: Sage.

Genocide The deliberate killing of a large group of people. Genocide is generally employed as a method of ethnic cleansing.

Reference

Danner, M. (1997). Ethnic cleansing in former Yugoslavia. *New York Review of Books*.

Haptics The study of our use of touch to communicate. Individuals within a culture vary as to the degree to which they touch while speaking. In communicating with various cultures, it is important to understand that each culture has a set of cultural conventions that guides who may touch whom, under what conditions, and where to touch. Haptic communication varies widely across culture, and the amount and kind of touch varies with age, sex, situation, and relationship of the people involved.

Reference

Jandt, F. (2007). *An introduction to intercultural communication: Identities in a global community* (5th ed.). Thousand Oaks, CA: Sage.

Heterosexism As with racist language, we see heterosexism in the derogatory terms used for lesbians and gay men as well as in more subtle forms of language usage (Devito, 2002). For example, when one qualifies a profession—as in gay athlete or lesbian doctor—this is in effect stating that athletes and doctors are not normally gay or lesbian. Further, this highlights the affectional orientation of the athlete and the doctor in a context in which it may have no relevance, in the same way that gender or racial distinctions offer no relevance to the issue at hand. Still another instance of heterosexism—and perhaps the most difficult to deal with—is the presumption of heterosexuality. Usually, people assume that the person they are talking to or about is heterosexual. They are usually correct because the majority of the population is heterosexual. At the same time, however, this assumption denies the LGBT identity a certain legitimacy. The practice is similar to the presumptions of whiteness and maleness that we have made significant inroads in eliminating.

Reference

Devito, J. (2002). *Essentials of human communication* (4th ed.). Boston: Allyn and Bacon.

Heterosexist language Refers to the language used to disparage LGBT members (Devito, 2002).

Reference

Devito, J. (2002). *Essentials of human communication* (4th ed.). Boston: Allyn and Bacon.

High contact cultures This refers to cultures that generally foster close physical relationships as a form of communication among its members. Edward Hall (1959) describes four types of contact: intimate, personal, social, and public. Examples of high contact cultures are Latin, Arabs, Greeks, Italians, French, and Turks. An example of low contact cultures would be some Asian cultures.

References

Hall, E.T. (1959). *The silent language.* Garden City, NY: Doubleday.
Madonik, B.G. (2001). *I hear what you say, but what are you telling me? The strategic use of nonverbal communication in mediation.* San Francisco: Jossey-Bass.

High context culture In this type of cultural environment members are expected to know how to perform, so information and cultural rules remain implicit. High context cultures rely on the context to convey a large part or even all of the message's meaning (Varner & Beamer, 1995). High context cultures have less tendency to trust words to communicate. They rely on context to help clarify and complete the message. Cultures in which less has to be said or written because more of the meaning is in the physical environment or already shared by people, are labeled high context. In high context cultures, most of the information is either in the physical context or internalized in the person. Very little is in the coded, explicit, transmitted part of the message (Jandt, 2004). High context communication refers to communication patterns of indirect verbal negotiation mode, and subtle nonverbal nuances. High context cultures, because of tradition and history, change very little over time. In the high context communication system, the listener or interpreter of the message is expected to "read between the lines," to accurately infer the implicit intent of the verbal message, and to decode the nonverbal subtleties that accompany the verbal message (Ting-Toomey & Chung, 2005). Cultures with high context communication systems are tradition bound—that is, their cultural traditions shape the behavior and lifestyle of group members, causing them to appear to be overly polite and indirect in relating others.

References

Jandt, F. (2004). *An introduction to intercultural communication: Identities in a global community* (4th ed.). Thousand Oaks, CA: Sage.
Ting-Toomey, S., & Chung, L. (2005). *Understanding intercultural communication.* Los Angeles: Roxbury.
Varner, I., & Beamer, L. (1995). *Intercultural communication: The global workplace.* Chicago: Irwin.

Hispanic According to Jandt (2004) the term Hispanic came into common use as a result of the 1980 census. This term has been used to identify various U.S. Spanish speakers who have a shared ancestry to Spain. Hispanic refers to that population segment with the capability of speaking and comprehending the Spanish language and whose ancestry is based in a Spanish-speaking country. The term has been rejected by some because its use was imposed by the government.

Reference

Jandt, F. (2004). *An introduction to intercultural communication: Identities in a global community* (4th ed.). Thousand Oaks, CA: Sage.

Homophobia This term is used to mean prejudice against homosexuals (Varner & Beamer, 1995). Jandt (2004) states that homophobia is related to heterosexism, the assumption that the world is and must be heterosexual, and patriarchy, the enforced belief in heterosexual male dominance and control. Homophobia is a learned attitude. Many historical studies have shown that homosexuals were not feared or despised in the past.

References

Jandt, F. (2004). *An introduction to intercultural communication: Identities in a global community* (4th ed.). Thousand Oaks, CA: Sage.

Varner, I., & Beamer, L. (1995). *Intercultural communication: The global workplace.* Chicago: Irwin.

> *Did you know...*
>
> It is illegal to be a prostitute in Siena, Italy, if your name is Mary.
> Human World: http://home.bitworks.co.nz/trivia/human.htm

I

Immigrant A person who leaves one country to permanently settle in another country.

Reference

American Heritage Dictionary of the English Language (4th ed.). (2000). Boston: Houghton Mifflin.

Immigration This is the act of foreigners moving into another country for permanent residence. Possible reasons for immigration include economic, political, family reunification, natural disaster, poverty, or the wish to change surroundings.

Reference

Booth, A. (1997). *Immigration and the family: Research and policy on U.S. immigrants.* Mahwah, NJ: Lawrence Erlbaum.

In-group/out-group In-group members are those who belong to particular groups. Examples of groups to which people belong are religion, sex, race, and social class. In-group privileges include recognition by other members, coded language, proximity, sympathy, and even empathy. In-group classification, therefore, determines out-group status. The circle that includes "us" excludes "them."

Reference

Brewer, M.B. (1979). In-group bias in the minimal inter-group situation: A cognitive-motivational analysis. *Psychological Bulletin, 86,* 307–324.

Individualism vs. collectivism Individualism concerns personal achievement (Dodd, 1998). Individualistic cultures are societies that value individual freedom, choice, uniqueness, and independence. These cultures place "I" before "we" and value competition over cooperation, private property over public or state-owned property, personal behavior over group behavior, and individual opinion over what anyone else might think. In individualistic cultures, members tend to join and belong to many groups, establishing a wide range of social relationships. Their attachment to these groups is apt to be weak, however, and their own personal goals take precedence over the group aims. In an individualistic culture, members are responsible for themselves and perhaps their immediate family (DeVito, 2001). People in individualistic culture tend to emphasize their self-concept in terms of self-esteem, self-identity, self-awareness, self-image, and self-expression. In other words, the individual is treated as the most important element in any social setting. Personal goals supersede group goals, and competition is often encouraged in this culture.

In contrast, collectivist cultures are those that emphasize community, groupness, harmony, and maintaining face (Dodd, 1998). Collectivists' cultures, on the other hand, value the group over the individual. These cultures place "we" before "I" and value commitment to family, tribe, and clan; their people tend to be loyal to spouse, employer, community, and country. According to Coleman (1998) as cited in Dodd (1998), collectivist cultures place a higher value on cooperation than on competition and on group-defined social norms and duties than on personal opinion (Dodd, 1998). Collectivistic cultures are characterized by a more rigid social framework in which self-concept plays a less significant role in social interactions (Chen & Starosta, 1998). In these cultures, people are expected to be interdependent and show conformity to the group's norms and values. In other words, the social networks are much more fixed and less reliant on the individual initiative.

References

Chen, G., & Starosta, W. (1998). *Foundations of intercultural communication*. Boston: Allyn and Bacon.

Devito, J. (2001). *The interpersonal communication book* (9th ed.). New York: Addison-Wesley Longman.

Dodd, C.H. (1998). *Dynamics of intercultural communication* (5th ed.). Boston: McGraw-Hill.

Jandt, F. (2004). *An introduction to intercultural communication: Identities in a global community* (4th ed.). Thousand Oaks, CA: Sage.

Klopf, D.W., & McCroskey, J.C. (2007). *Intercultural communication encounters*. Boston: Allyn and Bacon.

Samovar, L., Porter, R., & McDaniel, E. (2006). *Intercultural communication: A reader* (11th ed.). Belmont, CA: Thomson Wadsworth.

Ting-Toomey, S., & Chung, L. (2005). *Understanding intercultural communication*. Los Angeles: Roxbury.

Triantis, H.C. (1990). Cross-cultural studies of individualism and collectivism. In J.J. Berman (Ed.), *Cross cultural perspectives* (pp. 41–133). Lincoln, NE: University of Nebraska Press.

Wood, J. (1997). *Communication in our lives*. Belmont, CA: Wadsworth.

Institutional racism Is demonstrated when forces created through social institutions, structures, policies, precedents, and systems of social relations operate to deny certain racially identified groups their equal opportunities. Examples of institutional racism could result from an institution that denies access to an already disadvantaged group through exorbitant financial or educational requirements with or without intention to do so. Newman and Newman (1995) note that "social institutions such as family, church, school, business, and government create patterns of injustice and inequality based on the color of a person's skin."

Reference

Newman, G., & Newman, L.E. (1995). *Racism: Divided by color.* Springfield, NJ: Onslow.

Intercultural communication The exchange of messages by people of different cultures or subcultures (O'Hair et al., 1997). It is the circumstances in which people from diverse cultural backgrounds interact with one another (Samovar & Porter, 2004). Intercultural communication focuses on the study of the interaction between people from different cultural backgrounds, such as interactions between people from America and China (Chen & Starosta, 1998). When you speak to those with whom you have little or no cultural bond, you are engaging in intercultural communication (Berko, Wolvin, & Wolvin, 2004). To communicate successfully with members of another cultural group, we must be able to identify those behaviors that define the unique communication style of the culture. We must identify specific communicative behaviors, both those perceived as positive and those perceived as negative in a particular culture (Paratoo, 1993).

References

Berko, R., Wolvin, A., & Wolvin, D. (2004). *Communicating: A social and career focus* (9th ed.). Boston: Houghton Mifflin.

Chen, G., & Starosta, W. (1998). *Foundations of intercultural communication.* Boston: Allyn and Bacon.

Gamble, T., & Gamble, M. (2005). *Communication works* (8th ed.). Boston: Allyn and Bacon.

Nellie, J. (2003). *Intercultural communication: A contextual approach.* Boston: Houghton Mifflin.

O'Hair, D., Friedrich, G., Wiemann, J., & Wiemann, M. (1997). *Competent communication* (2nd ed.). New York: St. Martin's.

Paratoo, L. (1993). A pragmatic view on autonomous gestures: A first repot on cattalan emblems. *Journal of Pragmatics, 20,* 193–216.

Pearson, J., Nelson, P., Titsworth, S., & Harter L. (2006). *Human communication* (2nd ed.). New York: McGraw-Hill.

Samovar, L., & Porter, R. (2004). *Communication between cultures* (5th ed.). Belmont, CA: Wadsworth.

Ting-Toomey, S., & Chung, L. (2005). *Understanding intercultural communication.* Los Angeles: Roxbury.

Intercultural conflict The conflict between two or more cultural groups. Ting-Toomey and Oetzel (2001) state that "intercultural conflict often starts with different expectations concerning appropriate or inappropriate conflict behavior in a conflict scene."

Reference

Ting-Toomey, S., & Oetzel, J.G. (2001). *Managing intercultural conflict effectively.* Thousand Oaks, CA: Sage.

Intracultural communication When you interact with whom you have a cultural bond, you are participating in intracultural communication. For example, a baseball fan speaking to another baseball fan has a cultural bond (Berko, Wolvin, & Wolvin, 2004). Intracultural communication includes all forms of communication among members of the same racial, ethnic, or other co-culture or subculture group (Gamble & Gamble, 2005).

References

Berko, R., Wolvin, A., & Wolvin, D. (2004). *Communicating: A social and career focus* (9th ed.). Boston: Houghton Mifflin.

Gamble, T., & Gamble, M. (2005). *Communication works* (8th ed.). Boston: Allyn and Bacon.

Interracial communication Communication between races.

Reference

Devito, J. (1992). *The interpersonal communication book* (6th ed.). New York: HarperCollins.

Interethnic communication Communication between ethnic groups.

Reference

Devito, J. (1992). *The interpersonal communication book* (6th ed.). New York: HarperCollins.

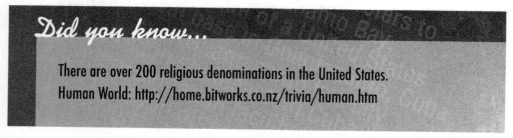

Did you know...

There are over 200 religious denominations in the United States.
Human World: http://home.bitworks.co.nz/trivia/human.htm

International communication Communication between nations (Devito, 1992). It focuses on the study of interaction between people from different cultural backgrounds, such as interactions between people from America and China (Chen & Starosta, 1998).

References

Chen, G., & Starosta, W. (1998). *Foundations of intercultural communication*. Boston: Allyn and Bacon.
Devito, J. (1992). *The interpersonal communication book* (6th ed.). New York: HarperCollins.

Integration When an individual or group retains its original cultural identity while seeking to maintain harmonious relationships with other cultures, integration occurs (Lustig & Koester, 2003). Integration produces distinguishable cultural groups that work cooperatively to ensure that the society and the individuals continue to function well. Both integration and assimilation promote harmony and result in an appropriate fit of individuals and groups to the larger culture. Jandt (2004) states that true integration is maintaining important parts of one's original culture as well as becoming an integral part of the new culture. Integration ensures the continuity of culture. The words *biculturalism* and *pluralism* have also been used to describe integration. The person feels as loyal to the country as to any ethnic group. Integration is supported by the dual-nationality trend, which allows expatriates from immigrant-sending nations to retain rights as nationals while taking citizenship status in the United States or elsewhere. In a seeming paradox, new U.S. citizens must formally renounce allegiances to foreign governments as part of the naturalization process, but U.S. law still permits citizens to possess other nationalities.

References

Jandt, F. (2004). *An introduction to intercultural communication: Identities in a global community* (4th ed.). Thousand Oaks, CA: Sage.
Lusting, M., & Koester, J. (2003). *Intercultural competence: Interpersonal communication across cultures* (4th ed.). Boston: Allyn and Bacon.

Integration of cultural differences Ability in integration enables a person not only to genuinely adapt to cultural difference but also to enjoy experiencing such differences in intercultural interactions (Chen & Starosta, 1998).

Reference

Chen, G., & Starosta, W. (1998). *Foundations of intercultural communication.* Boston: Allyn and Bacon.

K

Kwanzaa A secular festival observed by many African Americans from December 26 to January 1 as a celebration of their cultural heritage and traditional values. The celebration was founded by Maulanga Karenga of the U.S. Organization in 1966 as the first specifically African American holiday. This celebration upholds seven principles which represent family and social values.

References

Alexander, R. (1983). The evening hours. *New York Times.*
Karenga, R. M. (1972). *Kwanzaa.* Chicago: Institute of Positive Education.

L

Laotian The Laotian people are from the lowland country of Laos. Laos is a landlocked Southeast Asian country bordered by Burma, Thailand, Vietnam, Cambodia, and China. The 2010 U.S. census data puts the number of Laotians in the United States at 232,130. There has been an increase of approximately 65,000 Laotians since the 2000 census.

Reference

U.S. Census Bureau. http://2010.census.gov/2010census/about/

LGBT This abbreviation (also seen as GLBT) stands for Lesbian, Gay, Bisexual and Transgendered. It is used to represent the culture and community of people who assume any of the four or more self-identifying labels. In recent times the abbreviation has been expanded to include: **I** (for *intersex* persons born with congenital anomalies of sexual/reproductive anatomy, **Q** (for those who are *questioning* their sexual identity), and **A** (for those who are *allied* to the subculture—e.g., parents, siblings, friends, and others who support LGBT persons but are not themselves members of it).

References

Simpson College. (n.d.). LGBTQA. http://www.simpson.edu/mia/lgbtqa/index.html

University of California, Berkeley. (n.d.). LGBT resources: Definition of terms. Gender Equity Resource Center. http://geneq.berkeley.edu/lgbt_resources_definiton_of_terms

Low contact culture People from low contact cultures may feel uneasy when their personal space is invaded. Low contact cultures differ from high contact cultures in the amount of personal space that people require to feel comfortable (Gudykunst, 1998). Examples of low contact cultures include British, Japanese, and other Northern European cultures.

Reference

Gudykunst, W. (1998). *Bridging differences: Effective intergroup communication* (3rd ed.). Thousand Oaks, CA: Sage.

Low context culture In low context culture, information is explicit; procedures are explained; and expectations are discussed (Dodd, 1998). Context is not assumed to be understood, messages are explicit, direct, and completely encoded in words. Meaning is trusted almost entirely to words. Members of low context cultures put their thoughts into words (Varner & Beamer, 1995). They tend to suppose that if thoughts are not words, then the thoughts will not be understood correctly or completely. They think that when messages are in explicit words, the other side can act on them. Low context cultures are cultures in which little of the meaning is determined by the context because the message is encoded in the explicit code.

References

Dodd, C.H. (1998). *Dynamics of intercultural communication* (5th ed.). New York: McGraw Hill.

Jandt, F. (2004). *An introduction to intercultural communication: Identities in a global community* (4th ed.). Thousand Oaks, CA: Sage.

Varner, I., & Beamer, L. (1995). *Intercultural communication: The global workplace.* Chicago: Irwin.

Verderber, R., & Verdeber, S. (2005). *The challenge of effective speaking.* Boston: Wadsworth.

M

Machismo This is a Latino-American cultural value associated with the Latin male. According to Yep (1995), machismo is a gender role behavior that alludes to the assumed cultural expectation for men to be dominant in social relationships. Machismo can have both positive and negative connotations. As a positive attribute, machismo represents courage and responsibility. On the other hand, the negative aspects of machismo include behaviors such as being irresponsible, domineering, jealous, violent, insensitive to women, unfaithful, promiscuous, and abusive.

References

Castro, F. G., Proescholdbell, R.J., Albeita, L., & Rodriguez, D. (1999). *Ethnic and cultural minority groups.* In B.S. McCrady & E.E. Epstein (Eds.), *Additions: A comprehensive guide.* New York: Oxford University Press.

Sorenson, S.B., & Siegel, J.M. (1992). Gender, ethnicity and sexual assault: Findings from a Los Angeles study. *Journal of Social Issues, 48*, 93–104.

Yep, G.A. (1995). Communicating the HIV/AIDS risk to Hispanic populations: A review and integration. In A.M. Padilla (Ed.), *Hispanic psychology: Critical issues on theory and research.* Thousand Oaks, CA: Sage.

Macroculture The macroculture describes the predominant values and norms of a society. It consists of a set of values, formation of ideas, and symbols. According to Webster (1997), the United States is an example of a macroculture that consists of a number of microcultures; but representatives of any one of these microcultures can claim distinctiveness, autonomy, and educational rights.

Reference

Webster, Y. O. (1997). *Against the multicultural agenda: A critical thinking alternative.* Westport, CT: Prager.

Majority group A category of people within a society who possess distinct physical or cultural characteristics and maintain superior power and resources.

Reference

Doob, C.B. (2005). *Race, ethnicity, and the American urban mainstream*. Boston: Allyn and Bacon.

Marginality Marginality exists when sojourners get caught between two different cultures and do not clearly understand to which they belong (Chen & Starosta, 1998). The situation becomes ambiguous, and we are troubled by divided loyalties and uncertain self-identity. Social relationships for marginal sojourners tend to be functional and superficial with host nationals, rather than personal or intimate. As we remain reluctant to relinquish the major habits and customs of our own culture, our feeling of marginality often prevents us from appreciating or enjoying our own culture or that of the host.

Reference

Chen, G., & Starosta, W. (1998). *Foundations of intercultural communication*. Boston, MA: Allyn and Bacon.

Marginalization When individuals or groups neither retain their cultural heritage nor maintain positive contacts with other groups, marginalization occurs (Lustig & Koester, 2003). This form of adaptation is characterized by confusion and alienation. The choices of marginalization and separation are reactions to other cultures. The fit these outcomes achieve in the adaptation process is based on battling against, rather than working with, the other cultures in the social environment. Marginalization refers to losing one's cultural identity and not having any psychological contact with the larger society (Jandt, 2004). The person has feelings of not belonging anywhere.

References

Jandt, F. (2004). *An introduction to intercultural communication: Identities in a global community* (4th ed.). Thousand Oaks, CA: Sage.

Lusting, M., & Koester, J. (2003). *Intercultural competence: Interpersonal communication across cultures* (4th ed.). Boston: Allyn and Bacon.

Masculine vs. feminine culture Cultures differ in their attitude about gender role (Gamble & Gamble, 2005). Masculinity and femininity refers to the extent to which stereotypically masculine and feminine traits prevail in the culture (Chen & Starosta, 1998). The masculinity-femininity dimension describes how a culture's dominant values are assertive or nurturing. According to Adler and Rodman (2006) Hofstede uses the words *masculinity* and *femininity* to refer to the degree to which masculine or feminine traits are valued and revealed. "Masculine" and "feminine" also refer to the categories of task and social orientation, based on traditional views that men are assertive and results oriented, whereas women are nurturing.

The members of masculine cultures are socialized to be dominant and competitive (Gamble & Gamble, 2005). They tend to confront conflicts head-on and are likely to use a win–lose conflict strategy. Hofstede's masculine cultures are those that exhibit work as more central to their lives, strength, material success, assertiveness, and competitiveness (Dodd, 1998). Women are expected to serve and care for the nonmaterial aspects of life, for children, and for the weak. The varying degrees of masculinity and its values (e.g., assertiveness, performance, success, and competition) prevail over feminine values (Jandt, 2004).

In contrast, members of feminine cultures are more apt to compromise and negotiate in order to resolve conflicts, seeking win–win solutions (Gamble & Gamble, 2005). Feminine cultures are those that tend to accept fluid gender roles, embrace traits of affection, compassion, nurturing, and interpersonal relationships (Dodd, 1998). Feminine cultures perceive social roles as being overlapping for both men and women (Klopf & McCroskey, 2007). Neither men nor women need to be ambitious or competitive. Both sexes may opt for any sort of life not built on material success and may respect whatever is weak, small, and slow.

References

Adler, R., & Rodman, G. (2006). *Understanding human communication* (9th ed.). New York: Oxford University Press.

Chen, G., & Starosta, W. (1998). *Foundations of intercultural communication.* Boston: Allyn and Bacon.

Devito, J. (2001). *The interpersonal communication book* (9th ed.). New York: Addison-Wesley Longman.

Dodd, C.H. (1998). *Dynamics of intercultural communication* (5th ed.). Boston: McGraw-Hill.

Gamble, T., & Gamble, M. (2005). *Communication works* (8th ed.). Boston: Allyn and Bacon.

Jandt, F. (2004). *An introduction to intercultural communication: Identities in a global community* (4th ed.). Thousand Oaks, CA: Sage.

Klopf, D.W., & McCroskey, J.C. (2007). *Intercultural communication encounters.* Boston: Allyn and Bacon.

Samovar, L., Porter, R., & McDaniel, E. (2006). *Intercultural communication: A reader* (11th ed.). Belmont, CA: Thomson Wadsworth.

Ting-Toomey, S., & Chung, L. (2005). *Understanding intercultural communication.* Los Angeles: Roxbury.

Matriarchal This term is used to describe a society dominated by women. In a matriarchal society, power and property are handed down through the matrilineal descent (mother to daughter). This type of society is controlled by women or dominated by women with the traditional qualities of strength and assurance. One of the last remaining examples of matrilineal societies can be found in Mosuo, located in the Xiaolianghshan Mountains, in the Yunan province of South East China (Annitei, 1996).

Reference

Anitei, S. (1996). Mosuo, one of the last matriarchal societies. http://news.softpedia.com/news/Mosuo-One-of-the-Last-Matriarchal-Societies-36321.shtml

Melting pot concept The phase most often used to describe the assimilation of the early immigrants into the United States is "melting pot," which comes from Israel Zangwill's popular 1908 play, *The Melting Pot* (Jandt, 2004). The melting pot of old included English, German, Irish, French, and Italian immigrants and encouraged ethnic uniformity. Patriotic significance was placed on learning English and becoming "American." One seldom thinks of those of English, German, Irish, French, and Italian descent as "ethnic groups" because throughout the generations these groups have become assimilated into a somewhat homogenized society.

Reference

Jandt, F. (2004). *An introduction to intercultural communication: Identities in a global community* (4th ed.). Thousand Oaks, CA: Sage.

Middle Easterners Middle Easterners derive from Algeria, Bahrain, Egypt, Iran, Iraw, Israel, Jordan, Kuwait, Lebanon, Libya, Morocco, Oman, Qatar, Saudia Arabia, Syria, Tunisia, United Arab Emirates, Western Sahara, and Yemen (International Coalition, 2001).

Reference

International Coalition for Religious Freedom. (2001). *Religious freedom world report*. Silver Springs, MD: Author.

Minority group Any category of people with recognizable physical or cultural traits that place them in a position of restricted power and inferior status so that its members suffer limited opportunities and rewards. Minority group members are aware of their common oppression, and this awareness helps create a sense of belonging to the group. In some cases, the minority group is many times larger than the dominant group in the society.

Reference

Doob, C.B. (2005). *Race, ethnicity, and the American urban mainstream*. Boston: Allyn and Bacon.

Monogamy Originally the definition of monogamy was restricted to the tradition of marriage that involves one man and one woman. Monogamy is generally practiced in Western societies and may have been introduced into Christian philosophy to conform to Greek and Roman marriages. Based on recent social and legal changes, monogamy stands for exclusive relationships between two individuals.

Reference

Hall, L.E. (2005). *Dictionary of multicultural psychology: Issues, terms, and concepts*. Thousand Oaks, CA: Sage.

Did you know...

The two highest IQs ever recorded (on a standard test) both belong to women.
Human World: http://home.bitworks.co.nz/trivia/human.htm

Monolingual This term refers to individuals who speak one language. Ellis (2006) suggests that nations that speak the English language are both "the producers and beneficiaries of English as a global language" and the populations within these countries tend to be monolingual.

References

Ellis, E. (2006). *Monolingualism: The unmarked case.* Armidale, Australia: University of New England.
Merriam Webster Collegiate Dictionary. (1993). Springfield, MA: Merriam-Webster.

Multiculturalism The term multiculturalism became popular in the early 1980s mostly in the context of school reform (Erickson, 1992). Multiculturalism also means being tolerant toward racial minorities with regard to language, food, religion, and other cultural manifestations (Francis, 1998).

References

Erickson, P. (1992). What multiculturalism means. *Transition, 55*, 105–114.
Francis, S. (1998). The other face of multiculturalism. *Chronicles, 1*, 33.

Muslims A Muslim is a person who practices the religion of Islam which was founded by Mohhamed and considered one of the three great world religions. The term Muslim refers to a person who engages in the act of submission, acceptance, or surrender. Therefore, a Muslim is a person who submits to the will of God. Because Muslims are a minority community in many countries and most of the West, describing someone as a Muslim may also reflect on their lifestyle and choice of dress in addition to their religious beliefs. Current estimates conclude that the number of Muslims in the world is around 1.6 billion.

References

Difference between Islam and Muslim. http://www.differencebetween.net/miscellaneous/difference-between-islam-and-muslim/
Pew Research Center. (2011). *The future of the global Muslim population.*

Muted group theory A theory that suggests that individuals who do not belong to the dominant group are often silenced by a lack of opportunities to express their experiences, perceptions, and worldviews. The dominant group or "the majority" is defined as a cultural group that has primary access to institutional and economic power.

Reference

Lustig, M., & Koester, J. (2006). *Intercultural competence: Interpersonal communication across cultures* (5th ed.). Boston: Allyn and Bacon.

Native Americans According to Darlington (2011), the term Native American is used to represent the indigenous people of North America. As of 2010, there exists 564 federally recognized American Indian tribes and Alaska Natives in the United States (Bureau of Indian Affairs, 2010). The 2000 U.S. census reports that there are 2,475,956 people who are identified as either American Indian or Alaska Native.

References

Bureau of Indian Affairs. (2010). *United States Department of Interior.* Retrieved May 22, 2012, from http://www.bia.gov/index.htm

Darlington, Patricia St. E. (2011). *Cultural minority representation in the media: A historic view of television's underserved.* Dubuque, IA: Kendall-Hunt.

U.S. Census Bureau. (2000). *Census 2000 summary file.* Washington, DC: U.S. Census Bureau.

Nonverbal communication Lustig and Koester (2003) define nonverbal communication as a multichanneled process that is usually performed spontaneously; it typically involves a subtle set of nonlinguistic behaviors that are often enacted subconsciously. There are certain nonverbal tendencies which are performed by all humans. These include a smile, a head nod, and eye contact which may all have different meanings in different cultures.

Reference

Lustig, M.W., & Koester, J. (2003). *Intercultural competence: Interpersonal communication across cultures.* Boston: Allyn and Bacon, Pearson Publication.

Norms Socially constructed rules of behavior that tell us what is right/wrong or good/bad and when, where, or with whom we share these rules.

Reference

> Alloy, L., Jacobson, N., & Acocella, J. (1999). *Abnormal psychology: Current perspectives*. New York: McGraw Hill.

Did you know...

In Africa, there are over 1,000 languages spoken. Some of these languages are not written, only spoken.
Kulture Kids – Did You Know?: http://www.kulturekids.org/fun/didjaknow/index.html

O

Orientalism The process of labeling the peoples of "underdeveloped" cultures as insignificant "others."

Reference

> Jandt, F. (2007). *An introduction to intercultural communication: Identities in a global community* (5th ed.). Thousand Oaks, CA: Sage.

P

Personal identity This is an identity based on people's unique characteristics, which may differ from those of others in their cultural and social groups (Lustig & Koester, 2003). One may like cooking or chemistry, singing or sewing; one may play tennis or trombones, soccer or stereos; one may view oneself as studious or sociable, goofy or gracious; and most assuredly individuals have abilities, talents, quirks, and preferences that differ from those of others.

Reference

> Lusting, M., & Koester, J. (2003). *Intercultural competence: Interpersonal communication across cultures* (4th ed.). Boston: Allyn and Bacon.

Personal space According to Samovar and Porter (1997), personal space may be viewed as the way in which individuals expect the immediate space around them to be used. Lustig and Koester (2003) state that personal space distances are culture specific. People from colder climates tend to prefer larger distances while people from warmer climates prefer smaller distances.

References

Lusting, M., & Koester, J. (2003). *Intercultural competence: Interpersonal communication across cultures* (4th ed.). Boston: Allyn and Bacon.

Samovar, L.A., & Porter, R.E. (1997). *Intercultural communication: A reader.* London: Wadsworth Publishing Company.

Political correctness In its most basic form, it refers to the elimination of speech that oftentimes works to exclude, oppress, demean, or harass certain groups. Political correctness should increase one's awareness and sensitivity to the power of language when communicating with others.

Reference

Orbe, M.P., & Harris, T.M. (2001). *Interracial communication: Theory into practice.* Belmont, CA: Wadsworth.

Polygamy Polygamy refers to marriage in which a person may have several spouses concurrently. There are two primary aspects of polygamy: *Polygyny* refers to the union of one man and multiple wives; *polyandry* refers to the union of one woman and several husbands.

Reference

Hall, L.E. (2005). *Dictionary of multicultural psychology: Issues, terms, and concepts.* Thousand Oaks, CA: Sage.

Power distance Power distance measures the extent to which individuals are willing to accept power differences and status differences between members of a group (Gamble & Gamble, 2005). It is the degree of inequality among people which the population of a country considers as normal: from relatively equal to extremely unequal (Jandt, 2004).

References

Gamble, T., & Gamble, M. (2005). *Communication works* (8th ed.). Boston: Allyn and Bacon.

Jandt, F. (2004). *An introduction to intercultural communication: Identities in a global community* (4th ed.). Thousand Oaks, CA: Sage.

Prejudice In the intercultural context, prejudice is a sense of antagonistic hostility toward a group as a whole or toward an individual because she or he is a member of that group. Prejudice can be described as the possession of derogatory social attitudes or cognitive beliefs. Prejudice can result in negative affects and hostile or discriminatory behavior toward members of an out-group because of their membership in that group. We define prejudice, therefore, as a negative attitude directed to a group as a whole or to an individual member of that group (Klopf & McCroskey, 2007). Prejudice is a judgment that is based on emotion or some other irrational factor, but not on the facts (Varner & Beamer, 1995). Prejudice exists in spite of the facts. A prejudice is usually negative, and because it is not grounded in fact, it can be called an irrational bias. Prejudices often result from the insecurities and fears one has about the legitimacy or value of one's cultural group. Forming prejudices is a defense mechanism against groups that threaten one's (perceived) superiority.

References

Allport, G. (1954). *The nature of prejudice.* Cambridge, MA: Addison-Wesley.

Chen, G., & Starosta, W. (1998). *Foundations of intercultural communication.* Boston: Allyn and Bacon.

Jandt, F. (2004). *An introduction to intercultural communication: Identities in a global community* (4th ed.). Thousand Oaks, CA: Sage.

Klopf, D.W., & McCroskey, J.C. (2007). *Intercultural communication encounters* Boston: Allyn and Bacon

Lusting, M., & Koester, J. (2003). *Intercultural competence: Interpersonal communication across cultures* (4th ed.). Boston: Allyn and Bacon.

O'Hair, D., Friedrich, G., Wiemann, J., & Wiemann, M. (1997). *Competent communication* (2nd ed.). New York: St. Martin's.

Ting-Toomey, S., & Chung, L. (2005). *Understanding intercultural communication.* Los Angeles: Roxbury.

Varner, I., & Beamer, L. (1995). *Intercultural communication: The global workplace.* Chicago: Irwin.

R

Race There is extensive debate on the validity of racial classifications, and many people reject systems of racial classification as inherently arbitrary and subject to wide divergences in most populations due to the coexistence of ethnicities through conquests, invasions, migrations, and mass deportations, producing a heterogeneous world population. In general, however, the term race commonly refers to certain physical similarities, such as skin color or eye shape, that are shaped by a group of people and are used to mark or separate them from others (Lusting & Koester, 2003). Campbell (1976) defines race as a large body of people characterized by similarity of decent (Jandt, 2004).

References

Campbell, B.G. (1976). *Huamn-kind emerging.* Boston: Little, Brown.

Caucasian. (2000). In *Columbia encyclopedia.* New York: Columbia University Press.

Jandt, F. (2004). *An introduction to intercultural communication: Identities in a global community* (4th ed.). Thousand Oaks, CA: Sage.

Klopf, D.W., & McCroskey, J.C. (2007). *Intercultural communication encounters.* Boston: Allyn and Bacon

Lusting, M., & Koester, J. (2003). *Intercultural competence: Interpersonal communication across cultures* (4th ed.). Boston: Allyn and Bacon.

Racial groups Racial groups have generally been defined by genetically transmitted and inherited traits of physical appearance (Dodd, 1998). Examples include African Americans (or Blacks), Native Americans (or American Indians), and Asian Americans.

Reference

Dodd, C.H. (1998). *Dynamics of intercultural communication* (5th ed.). Boston: McGraw-Hill.

Did you know...

Dreadlocked hair was worn in ancient Crete around 3000–1400 BCE.
Kulture Kids – Did You Know?: http://www.kulturekids.org/fun/didjaknow/index.html

Racialized social system A social system in which people's racial classification partially determines their access to valued economic, political, and social resources. The key of such a system's survival is the maintenance of a pattern of racial imbalance, in which many members of the majority group are in superordinate roles, and in turn, racial minorities primarily remain in subordinate locations.

Reference

Doob, C.B. (2005). *Race, ethnicity, and the American urban mainstream*. Boston: Allyn and Bacon.

Racism Racism is any policy, practice, belief, or attitude that attributes characteristics or status to individuals based on their race (Jandt, 2004). Racism involves not only prejudice but the exercise of power over individuals based on their race. Racism ranges from forms that are almost impossible to detect to signs that are blatant and transparent (Samovar & Porter, 2004). Four of the most common forms are intense racism, symbolic racism, tokenism, and arm's length racism.

Intense racism—This form of racism begins with the belief that certain people (those of a race different from the person making and drawing the conclusion) are inferior, and hence are perceived as being of low worth.

Symbolic racism—Refers to out-groups as devalued not because of inherent inferiority, but because the group is seen as blocking basic cultural goals (Dodd, 1998).

Tokenism—Whether it be in the form of prejudice or racism, tokenism is difficult to detect. In this case the person does not want to admit that he or she harbors negative or racist views. People will even engage in "token" activities to "prove" they are even-handed in the treatment of other races.

Arm's length racism—Suggests that some people engage in friendly, positive behaviors toward out-group members in some social settings but treat those same out-group members with noticeably less warmth and friendliness in other settings.

References

Dodd, C.H. (1998). *Dynamics of intercultural communication* (5th ed.). Boston: McGraw-Hill.

Essed, P. (1991). *Understanding everyday racism.* Newbury Park, CA: Sage.

Jandt, F. (2004). *An introduction to intercultural communication: Identities in a global community* (4th ed.). Thousand Oaks, CA: Sage.

Macionis, J.J. (1998). *Society: The basics* (4th ed.). Upper Saddle River, NJ: Prentice Hall.

Rothenberg, P.S. (Ed.). (1992). *Race, class, and gender in the united sates: An integrated study* (2nd ed.). New York: St. Martin's.

Samovar, L., & Porter, R. (2004). *Communication between cultures* (5th ed.). Belmont,CA: Wadsworth.

Van Dijk, T.A. (1987). *Communication racism: Ethnic prejudice in thought and talk.* Newbury Park, CA: Sage.

Varner, I., & Beamer, L. (1995). *Intercultural communication: The global workplace.* Chicago: Irwin.

Racist language Racist language emphasizes differences rather than similarities and separates rather than unites members of different cultures. Traditionally, racist language has been used by the dominant group to establish and maintain power over other groups. Today, however, it is used by racists (or the racist-talking) in all groups. The social consequences of racist language in terms of employment, education, housing opportunities, and general community acceptance are well known (Devito, 1992, p. 168). *Racist terms* or *racist expressions* are used by members of one culture to disparage members of other cultures—their customs or their accomplishments. Racist terms reinforce the negative stereotypes that one cultural group has assigned to another cultural group (Devito, 1992).

References

Devito, J. (1992). *The interpersonal communication book* (6th ed.). New York: HarperCollins.

Devito, J. (2001). *Essentials of human communication* (4th ed.). Boston: Allyn and Bacon.

Rich, A. L. (1974). *Interracial communication.* New York: Harper & Row.

Redlining The discriminatory practice of refusing to provide mortgage loans or property insurance or only providing them at accelerated rates for reasons not clearly associated with any conventional assessment of risk.

Reference

Doob, C.B. (2005). *Race, ethnicity, and the American urban mainstream.* Boston: Allyn and Bacon.

Refugee Refugees are people who have fled to another country or have been expelled and cannot return due to fear of persecution, war, or natural disasters. Refugees are not the same as immigrants, who leave their country by choice.

Reference

> United Nations High Commission for Refugees. (2012). Convention relating to the status of refugees. http://www2.ohchr.org/english/law/refugees.htm

Did you know...

The three most common languages in the world are Mandarin Chinese, Spanish, and English. Great Facts.com: http://www.greatfacts.com/

S

Seclusion When a nondominant group chooses not to participate in the larger society in order to retain its own way of life.

Reference

> Lusting, M., & Koester, J. (2003). *Intercultural competence: Interpersonal communication across cultures* (4th ed.). Boston: Allyn and Bacon.

Segregation When separation occurs because the more politically and economically powerful culture does not want the intercultural contact.

Reference

> Lusting, M., & Koester, J. (2003). *Intercultural competence: Interpersonal communication across cultures* (4th ed.). Boston: Allyn and Bacon.

Separation When individuals or groups do not want to maintain positive relationships with members of other groups, the outcomes are starkly different (Lustig & Koester, 2003). If a culture a does not want positive relationships with another culture and it also wishes to retain its cultural characteristics, separation may result. On the other hand, when members of a co-culture resist interacting with members of the dominant culture, they employ the strategy of resistance, or separation (Gamble & Gamble, 2005). Because these persons, such as Hassidic Jews, prefer to interact with each other rather than have contact with persons they perceive to be outsiders, they tend to keep to themselves. Pearson and colleagues (2006) believe that separation is achieved when the marginalized group relates as exclusively as possible with its own group and as little as possible with the dominant group (e.g., Hasidic Jews, the Amish). Marginalized individuals can live separate lives in the midst of the dominant culture by relentless focus on work, studiously avoiding any but the most necessary interaction, and by never socializing outside work with any colleagues.

References

Gamble, T., & Gamble, M. (2005). *Communication works* (8th ed.). Boston: Allyn and Bacon.

Lusting, M., & Koester, J. (2003). *Intercultural competence: Interpersonal communication across cultures* (4th ed.). Boston: Allyn and Bacon.

Pearson, J., Nelson, P., Titsworth, S., & Harter L. (2006). *Human communication* (2nd ed.). New York: McGraw-Hill.

Separation and segregation This refers to maintaining one's original culture and not participating in the new culture (Jandt, 2004). To some, segregation connotes a judgment of superiority, and inferiority and prejudice, and hatred between groups. Others use the term *insularity* to connote separation only. The person has a strong sense of ethnic identity (Jandt, 2004, p. 337).

Reference

Jandt, F. (2004). *An introduction to intercultural communication: Identities in a global community* (4th ed.). Thousand Oaks, CA: Sage.

Sex Sex is the most used term to refer to the biological features that distinguish men from women (Jandt, 2004). The word *gender* is most often used to refer to the learned behaviors and attitudes associated with the words *feminine* and *masculine*. Traits that are considered feminine are attributes such as affection, compassion, nurturance, and emotionality. Traits that are considered masculine are typically attributes such as strength, assertiveness, competitiveness, and ambitiousness.

Reference

Jandt, F. (2004). *An introduction to intercultural communication: Identities in a global community* (4th ed.). Thousand Oaks, CA: Sage.

Sex-role stereotyping The assumption that certain roles or professions belong to men and others belong to women. In eliminating sex-role stereotyping, avoid for example, making the hypothetical elementary school teacher female and the college professor male. Avoid referring to doctors as male and nurses as female. Avoid noting the sex of a professional with terms such as "female doctor" or "male nurse." When you're referring to a specific doctor or nurse, the person's sex will become clear when you use the appropriate pronoun: "Dr. Smith wrote the prescription for her new patient" or "The nurse recorded the patient's temperature himself" (Devito 2002, p. 170).

References

Devito, J. (2001). *The interpersonal communication book* (9th ed.). New York: Addison-Wesley Longman.
Devito, J. (2002). *Essentials of human communication* (4th ed.). Boston: Allyn and Bacon.
Pearson, J., Nelson, P., Titsworth, S., & Harter, L. (2006). *Human communication* (2nd ed.). New York: McGraw-Hill.
Penfield, J. (Ed.). (1987). *Women and language in transition*. Albany, NY: State University of New York Press.

Sexism Term for limiting women to traditional women's roles and men to traditional men's roles (Jandt, 2004). It is the opinion that one gender is superior over another (Varner & Beamer, 1995).

References

Jandt, F. (2004). *An introduction to intercultural communication: Identities in a global community* (4th ed.). Thousand Oaks, CA: Sage.
Varner, I., & Beamer, L. (1995). *Intercultural communication: The global workplace*. Chicago: Irwin.

Did you know...

In 1865, the U.S. Secret Service was first established for the specific purpose to combat the counterfeiting of money.
Great Facts.com: http://www.greatfacts.com/

Sexist language This is language that excludes individuals on the basis of gender (Pearson et al., 2006). Devito (2002) says that it is language that puts down someone because of her or his gender. Usually, the term refers to language that denigrates women, but it can also legitimately refer to language that denigrates men. Usually, sexist language is used by one sex against the other, but it need not be limited to these cases; women can be sexist against women and men can be sexist against men.

References

Devito, J. (2001). *The interpersonal communication book* (9th ed.). New York: Addison-Wesley Longman.

Devito, J. (2002). *Essentials of human communication* (4th ed.). Boston: Allyn and Bacon.

Pearson, J., Nelson, P., Titsworth, S., & Harter, L. (2006). *Human communication* (2nd ed.). New York: McGraw-Hill.

Penfield, J. (Ed.). (1987). *Women and language in transition.* Albany, NY: State University of New York Press.

Short- vs. long-term orientation According to Adler and Rodman (2006), members of some cultures look for quick payoffs, whereas members of other cultures are willing to defer gratification in pursuit of long-range goals. The willingness to work hard today for future payoff is especially common in East Asian cultures including China, Japan, and South Korea. Western industrialized cultures are much more focused on short-term results. In subsequent research, a fifth dimension of national culture differences has been found (Jandt, 2004). Professor Michael H. Bond of the Chinese University of Hong Kong studied value differences among students in twenty-three different countries using a questionnaire originally designed in the Chinese language by Chinese scholars. Analysis of the data produced four dimensions, three of them very similar to three of the IBM dimensions (all except uncertainty avoidance), the fourth entirely new and very meaningful (p. 11). The fifth dimension was called long-term orientation (LTO) as opposed to short-term orientation. Values positively rated in LTO are thrift and perseverance; values negatively related are respect for tradition and fulfilling social expectations—that is, "keeping up with the Joneses" (p. 11). This fifth dimension was also identified by Hofstede, along with Bond (1984). The Confucian dynamism dimension describes cultures that range from short-term values with respect to tradition and reciprocity in social relations to long-term values with persistence and ordering relationships by status.

References

Adler, R., & Rodman, G. (2006). *Understanding human communication* (9th ed.). New York: Oxford University Press.

Hofstede, G., & Bond, M.H. (1984). Hofstede's cultural dimensions: An independent validation using Rokeach's value survey. *Journal of Cross-Cultural Psychology*, 15.

Jandt, F. (2004). *An introduction to intercultural communication: Identities in a global community* (4th ed.). Thousand Oaks, CA: Sage.

Skin color Research in the United States on prejudice shows that skin color is the most salient characteristic that influences people's perception and judgment of each other (Samovar & Porter, 2004). Students with a lighter skin color tend to be more acceptable to teachers in multicultural classroom settings. Studies of classroom interaction in the United States (Bennett, 1990) have also demonstrated that teachers have high expectations for and communicate more frequently with White students or those with a lighter complexion (than with a Black, Hispanic, or other darker-skinned student). Although these teachers might be unaware of their unequal and dualistic treatment of students, they have accepted the racist view that a student's physical traits determine his or her social behavior, intellectual abilities, and personality traits. This rigid form of prejudiced social judgment affects the formation of social relations in the classroom and impacts negatively on minority culture children's self-concepts and school achievement (p. 345).

References

Bennett, C.I. (1990). *Multicultural education: Theory and practice.* Boston: Allyn and Bacon.

Samovar, L., & Porter, R. (2004). *Communication between cultures* (5th ed.). Belmont, CA.: Wadsworth.

Did you know...

The first couple to be shown on a sitcom sleeping in the same bed was Mary Kay and Johnny (1947–1950).
Great Facts.com: http://www.greatfacts.com/

Social identity Social identity develops as a consequence of memberships in particular groups within one's culture. The types of groups with which people identify can vary widely and might include perceived similarities due to age, gender, work, religion, ideology, social class, place (neighborhood, region, and nation), and common interests. For instance, those baseball players, ballet dancers, and scientists who strongly identify with their particular professions likely view themselves as "belonging" to "their" group of professionals, with whom they have similar traits and share similar concerns (Lusting & Koester, 2003, p. 141).

Reference

Lusting, M., & Koester, J. (2003). *Intercultural competence: Interpersonal communication across cultures* (4th ed.). Boston: Allyn and Bacon.

Social relations orientation According to Dr. A.M. Kanu, "The social relations orientation describes how people in a culture organize themselves and relate to one another. This orientation provides answers to questions such as: To what extent are some people in the culture considered better or superior to others?" This orientation also relates to issues of equality and hierarcy in social settings.

Reference

Kanu, A.M. (2012, April 24). Relational communication and social orientation. Retrieved from http://www.articlesbase.com/culture-articles/relational-communication-and-social-orientations-5851006.html.

Social system A society's fairly enduring set of interrelated institutions (involving the economy, the family, political order, education, and so forth) that the society's elite seeks to control, both to maximize their own interests and to ensure their citizens' survival and reproduction.

Reference

Doob, C.B. (2005). *Race, ethnicity, and the American urban mainstream*. Boston: Allyn and Bacon.

Socialization Culture is a power vehicle for socialization (Dodd, 1998). Culture influences how we adapt and learn language, habits, customs, expectations, and roles; it shapes thinking, acting, and communicating according to group expectations. Many cultural imprints are subtle and elusive, if not beyond conscious recognition at times. Culture is so basic to human behavior that we cannot ignore its pervasive influence in recent years in regard to communication research (p. 36). It is important to understand the overall reason why culture influences communication. Culture teaches significant rules, rituals, and procedures. Attitudes toward time, how and when to dress, when and what to eat, when to come and go, and how to work illustrate this first function of culture. The overall process of learning these things is called socialization—which refers to developing a sense of proper and improper behavior and communicating within those cultural rules (see footnote 1). As an example think over any one of thousands of rules your culture or your family may have taught you. What is polite, crude, or expected all fall under the rubric of rules, rituals, and procedures (p. 36).

References

Devito, J. (1992). *The interpersonal communication book* (6th ed.). New York: HarperCollins.

Dodd, C.H. (1998). *Dynamics of intercultural communication* (5th ed.). Boston: McGraw-Hill

Standpoint theory This theory is based on the premise that our perceptions of the world around us are largely influenced by social group membership. Our set of life experiences will shape, and are shaped by, our membership with different cultural groups, like those based on sex, race/ethnicity, and sexual orientation. In explicit and implicit ways, our standpoints affect how we communicate as well as how we perceive the communication of others.

Reference

Orbe, M.P., & Harris, T.M. (2001). *Interracial communication: Theory into practice.* Belmont, CA: Wadsworth.

Stereotypes Allport states that stereotypes are the overgeneralized and oversimplified beliefs we use to categorize a group of people (as cited in Chen & Starosta, 1998, p. 39). Stereotype is the broader term commonly used to refer to negative or positive judgments made about individuals based on observable or believed group membership (Jandt, 2004). We have a tendency to make a claim that often goes beyond the facts, with no valid basis. Stereotypes may be based on the truth, but they are exaggerated statements regarding our belief about what a group of people are or should be. For example, imagine that your wallet was stolen by "a" Korean when you were traveling in Korea last summer. The incident ruined your whole trip there. When you came back, your friends asked how your trip to Korea was. You have said, "Those Koreans are thieves. They stole my wallet." This is an example of stereotyping. We form stereotypes in three ways. First, we may categorize a people or things by the most obvious characteristics they possess. Second, we may apply a set of characteristics to a whole group of people. For example, you may hear someone say that Americans eat hotdogs and wear cowboy boots. Third, we may give the same treatment to each member of the group. "You are a Chinese, you must be smart" is stereotyping (p. 39). Stereotypes may be accurate or inaccurate. In some cases, we have incorrect understandings of a group, and in other cases some members of a group don't conform to the behaviors we think are typical of the group as a whole. Although we need stereotypes in order to predict what will happen, we should remember that they are selective, subjective, and not necessarily complete or accurate (Wood, 2006, p. 48).

References

Chen, G., & Starosta, W. (1998). *Foundations of intercultural communication*. Boston: Allyn and Bacon.

Devito, J. (2002). *Essentials of human communication* (4th ed.). Boston: Allyn and Bacon.

Goodall Jr., H.L., & Goodall, S. (2006). *Communicating in professional contexts: Skills, ethics, and technologies* (2nd ed.). Belmont, CA: Thomson Wadsworth.

Jandt, F. (2004). *An introduction to intercultural communication: Identities in a global community* (4th ed.). Thousand Oaks, CA: Sage.

O'Hair, D., Friedrich, G., Wiemann, J., & Wiemann, M. (1997). *Competent communication* (2nd ed.). New York: St. Martin's.

Pearson, J., Nelson, P., Titsworth, S., & Harter, L. (2006). *Human communication* (2nd ed.). New York: McGraw-Hill.

Remland, M.S. (2000). *Nonverbal communication in everyday life*. Boston: Houghton Mifflin College Division.

Samovar, L., & Porter, R. (2004). *Communication between cultures* (5th ed.). Belmont, CA: Wadsworth.

Wood, J. (1997). *Communication in our lives*. Belmont, CA: Wadsworth.

Wood, J. (2006). *Communication mosaics: An introduction to the field of communication* (4th ed.). Belmont, CA: Thomson Wadsworth.

Subcultures Gamble and Gamble (2005) state that co-cultures or subcultures are composed of members of the same general culture who differ in some ethnic or sociological way from the parent culture. In our society, African Americans, Hispanic Americans, Japanese Americans, the disabled, gays and lesbians, and the elderly are just some of the co-cultures belonging to the same general culture. Subcultures is used to refer to groups within a larger culture that are distinguished from the rest of the population by various characteristics (O'Hair et al., 1997). For example, white Protestant males and African American Catholic females constitute two subcultures in the United States. They are co-cultures of each other.

References

Gamble, T., & Gamble, M. (2005). *Communication works* (8th ed.). Boston: Allyn and Bacon.

O'Hair, D., Friedrich, G., Wiemann, J., & Wiemann, M. (1997). *Competent communication* (2nd ed.). New York: St. Martin's.

Did you know...

At least 2.5 cans of Spam are consumed every second in the United States.
Great Facts.com: http://www.greatfacts.com/

T

Third World According to Tomlinson (2003), over the last few decades the term Third World has been used interchangeably with the terms "Global South" and "Developing Countries" to describe poorer countries that have struggled to attain steady economic development. The term was originally used to describe the more than 100 economically underdeveloped nations in Asia, Africa, South America, and the Caribbean (Elliott, 1991).

References

Elliott, J. M. (1991). *Annual editions: Third world 91/92*. Guilford, CT: Dushkin.

Tomlinson, B.R. (2003). What was the third world. *Journal of Contemporary History*, *38*(2): 307–321.

𝒰

U-curve model A theory of adaptation positing that migrants go through fairly predictable phases—excitement/anticipation, shock/disorientation, and adjustment—in adapting to a new cultural situation.

Reference

Lustig, M., & Koester, J. (2006). *Intercultural competence: Interpersonal communication across cultures* (5th ed.). Boston: Allyn and Bacon.

𝒲

Worldview Hellman (1996) compared the term worldview to culture. He describes it as "a set of guidelines [both explicit and implicit] which individuals inherit as members of a particular society, and which tells them how to *view* the world, how to experience it *emotionally*, and how to *behave* in it in relation to other people, to supernatural forces or gods, and to the natural environment" (pp. 2–3). On the other hand, Hall (1995) defines worldview as "abstract notions about the way the world is." He suggests that worldviews are "not open for challenge or debate. In fact they are usually the premises upon which challenges and debates are conducted."

References

Hall, B.J. (2005). *Among cultures: The challenge of communication*. Belmont, CA: Thomson Wadsworth.

Hellman, C.G. (1996) *Culture, health and illness*. Oxford: Butterworth-Heinemann

𝒳

Xenophobia The term *xenos* is Greek for "stranger," and *phobos* is Greek for "fear." Thus, the term xenophobia refers to the fear of the stranger, the other, the unknown (Allen, 1993).

Reference

Allen, D. (1993). *Fear of strangers: And its consequences*. Grawn, MI: Bennington.

PART 2

Political and Pop Culture Terms

1 percent (1%) A term used to denote the segment of the U.S. population whose net worth classifies them as the top 1% of income earners in the country. The term was first used by participants of the Occupy Wall Street movement as a disparaging way to identify the segment of society that, according to the movement, benefits from certain governmental policies, leaving the remaining 99% of the population in less advantageous positions. The average net worth of a 1-percenter is 70 times that of the average American.

Reference

Dunn, A. (2012, March 21). Average America vs the one percent. *Forbes*. Retrieved from http://www.forbes.com/sites/moneywisewomen/2012/03/21/average-america-vs-the-one-percent/

527 A tax-exempt group organized under section 527 of the Internal Revenue Code to raise money for political activities including voter mobilization efforts, issue advocacy, and the like.

Reference

Types of advocacy groups. (2012). Retrieved from http://www.opensecrets.org/527s/types.php

99 percent (99%) A term used to denote the segment of the U.S. population whose net worth classifies them as lower-level income earners in the country. The term was first used by participants of the Occupy Wall Street movement as a way to identify the segment of society that, according to the movement, is significantly disadvantaged by certain governmental policies, to the benefit of those identified as the 1-percenters. The average net worth of a 1-percenter is 70 times that of the average American.

Reference

Dunn, A. (2012, March 21). Average America vs the one percent. *Forbes*. Retrieved from http://www.forbes.com/sites/moneywisewomen/2012/03/21/average-america-vs-the-one-percent/

Did you know...

Instead of a birthday cake, many Russian children are given a birthday pie.
Great Facts.com: http://www.greatfacts.com/

9-9-9 A tax policy proposed during the 2012 Republican presidential primary race, by candidate Herman Cain. This policy proposed that the federal government collect three categories of taxes from the American people: a 9% federal sales tax, a 9% personal income tax, and a 9% business transaction tax.

Reference

Gabriel, T., & Saulny, S. (2011, October 12). With just three 9s, Cain refigured math for taxes. *The New York Times*. Retrieved from http://www.nytimes.com/2011/10/13/us/politics/herman-cains-tax-plan-changes-gop-primary-math.html?_r=1

A

Al-Qaeda An international organization of loosely affiliated cells (groups of individuals) that carry out attacks and bombings in the attempt to disrupt the economies and influence of Western nations and advance Islamic fundamentalism. According to Globalsecurity.org, al-Qaeda's current goal is to establish a pan-Islamic caliphate throughout the world by working with allied Islamic extremist groups to overthrow regimes it deems "non-Islamic" and expelling Westerners and non-Muslims from Muslim countries.

Reference

> Pike, J. (2012, March 26). *Al-Qaida/Al-Qaeda*. Retrieved from http://www.globalsecurity.org/military/world/para/al-qaida.htm

Appropriation The setting aside of legislated funds for the purpose of implementing and maintaining that piece of legislation. The federal government allocates funds specifically for government programs.

Reference

> Investopedia. (2012). *Appropriation*. Retrieved from http://www.investopedia.com/terms/a/appropriation.asp#axzz1w2Nq1nHB

Austerity Policies undertaken by a government in an effort to reduce a budget deficit, which can include drastic spending cuts, cuts to salaries and benefits, tax increases, and funding roll-backs, for the purpose of regaining and sustaining economic prosperity.

Reference

> Investopedia. (2012). *Austerity*. Retrieved from http://www.investopedia.com/terms/a/austerity.asp

Big tent politics A term used to refer to a style of politics which aims to expand the electorate, population, or demographic groups to which it appeals, and to encourage membership of those who may not agree with all parts of the party's ideology.

Reference

> Big tent. (n.d.). In *Macmillan dictionary online*. Retrieved from http://www.macmillandictionary.com/dictionary/american/big-tent

Birther(s) A term used to describe individuals who believe that President Barack Obama is not a natural born U.S. citizen—a requirement for eligibility for the presidency of the United States of America. These individuals maintain their doubt despite documentation proffered by official from the president's birth state, Hawaii. As a result of their doubt, birthers challenge the legitimacy of Obama's presidency.

Reference

Birther. (n.d.). In *Macmillan dictionary online*. Retrieved from http://www.macmillandictionary.com/buzzword/entries/birther.html

Blog A personal journal published on the World Wide Web consisting of entries called "posts," which are usually accessed in reverse chronological order so that the most recent post appears first. Blogs are usually the work of a single individual or a small group, and often are themed on a single subject. The word blog is a contraction of the words *web* and *log*.

Reference

Blood, R. (2000, September 7). Weblogs: A history and perspective. *Rebecca's pocket*. Retrieved from http://www.rebeccablood.net/essays/weblog_history.html

Blogosphere A term used to refer to the collective of all blogs and their interconnections, implying that all blogs exist together as a collection of connected communities or social networks in which any blogger can publish their opinions. The term has been offered as a conjunction showing the interaction in the public sphere thru weblogs.

References

Baoill, A. (n.d.). *Weblogs and the public sphere. Into the blogosphere: Rhetoric, community, and culture of weblogs*. Retrieved from http://blog.lib.umn.edu/blogosphere/weblogs_and_the_public_sphere.html

Blogosphere. (n.d.). In *Merriam-Webster online dictionary* (11th ed.). Retrieved from http://www.merriam-webster.com/dictionary/blogosphere

Buffett rule A change in the tax code designed to ensure that the wealthiest Americans do not pay a lower share of their income in taxes than members of the middle class. This rule was inspired and championed by mega-investor Warren Buffett's revelation that he pays a lower percentage of income tax on his earnings than his secretary did on her salary.

Reference

Leonard, A. (2011). The Buffett rule, explained. *Salon*. Retrieved from http://www.salon.com/2012/04/11/the_buffet_rule_explained/

C

Campaign finance reform This term defines the political effort in the United States to change the involvement of money in politics, primarily in political campaigns. The Federal Election Campaign Act (FECA) of 1972 required candidates to disclose sources of campaign contributions and campaign expenditures. It was amended in 1974 with the introduction of statutory limits on contribution, and creation of the Federal Election Commission (FEC). A recent legislative attempt at Campaign Finance Reform was addressed by the U.S. Supreme Court in its 2010 Citizen's United ruling.

Reference

Campaign finance. (n.d.). Retrieved from http://www.govspot.com/issues/campaignfinance.htm

Captured agency A term used to refer to a governmental agency that works in ways that favor the very industry it is charged to regulate, instead of implementing and enforcing regulations otherwise appropriate for the given agency.

Reference

University of Texas. (n.d.). *Political economy and public policy glossary.* Retrieved from http://www.laits.utexas.edu/gov310/PEP/glossary.html

Caucus A group of elected congressional members who represent a particular interest or demographic among the representatives. Some of the most recognizable causes in the U.S. Congress are the Democratic caucus, the Republican caucus, the Congressional Black caucus, and the Tea Party caucus.

Reference

Bureau of International Information Programs, U.S. Department of State. (2007, October 9). *Glossary: Caucus.* Retrieved from http://www.america.gov/st/pubs-english/2007/October/20071009122700hmnietsua0.2381555.html

Caucus A meeting specially arranged by either a state or political party in which registered members of a political party in a city, town, or county gather to express support for a candidate. For statewide or national offices, those recommendations are combined to determine the state party nominee. Unlike primary voting which is done by secret ballot, caucus voting is open, enabling participants to openly show support for candidates. Voting is often done by raising hands or breaking into groups according to the participants' support of their candidate.

References

Bureau of International Information Programs, U.S. Department of State. (2007, October 9). *Glossary: Caucus.* Retrieved from http://www.america.gov/st/pubs-english/2007/October/20071009122700hmnietsua0.2381555.html

Gore, D. (2008, April 8). *Caucus vs. primary.* Retrieved from http://www.factcheck.org/2008/04/caucus-vs-primary/

Did you know...

Native Indians have been known to paint their doors blue, which they believe keeps the bad spirits out.
Great Facts.com: http://www.greatfacts.com/

Challenger A candidate in a political race who runs in opposition to the incumbent candidate.

Reference

Incumbent. (2006). In *Merriam-Webster's collegiate dictionary* (11th ed.). Springfield, MA: Merriam-Webster.

Citizen's United In a 5-4 decision, the U.S. Supreme Court ruled that corporations and unions have the same political speech rights as individuals under the First Amendment, and therefore could contribute to political campaign fundraising efforts for specific candidates.

Reference

Sullivan, K., & Adams, T. (2010). *Summary of Citizens v. Federal Election Commission*. Retrieved from http://www.cga.ct.gov/2010/rpt/2010-R-0124.htm

Class warfare A term, while present in American political discourse for decades, has taken on a divisive connotation and has come to represent issues surrounding tax reform, income inequality, entitlements, income gaps, and the growing disparity between the wealthiest and poorest citizens in American society. Also see **Buffet rule.**

Reference

Stein, B. (2006, November 26). In class warfare, guess which class is winning. *The New York Times*. Retrieved from http://www.nytimes.com/2006/11/26/business/yourmoney/26every.html

Closed primary A primary contest that is closed to voters who are not registered as a member of the party offering the election.

Reference

Closed primary. (n.d.). In *Merriam-Webster online dictionary* (11th ed.). Retrieved from http://www.merriam-webster.com/dictionary/closed%20primary

Cloture The only procedure by which the Senate can vote to limit the time allowed for consideration of a bill or other matter, and thereby overcome a filibuster. Under this rule the Senate may limit considerations to 30 additional hours, but only by a vote of three-fifths of the full Senate, normally 60 votes.

Reference

United States Senate. (2012). *Glossary: Cloture.* Retrieved from http://www.senate. gov/reference/glossary_term/cloture.htm

Conference committee A temporary, ad hoc panel composed of House and Senate conferees which is formed for the purpose of reconciling differences in legislation that has passed both chambers. Conference committees are usually convened to resolve bicameral differences between major and controversial legislation.

References

United States Senate. (2012). *Glossary: Conference committee.* Retrieved from http:// www.senate.gov/reference/glossary_term/conference_committee.htm

Conservative A political movement that is commonly associated with ideologies like individual responsibility, individual liberty, tradition, the rule of law, limited government, free market principals, a strong national defense, family values, and Judaic-Christian history. While this term has morphed considerably in the 20th century, its foundational ideals remain. Often used interchangeably with Republicanism.

Reference

Conservative vs. liberal beliefs. (2010). Retrieved May 28, 2012 from http://www.studentnewsdaily.com/conservative-vs.-liberal-beliefs/

Death panels A disparaging term created to refer to provisions in the Patient Protection and Affordable Care Act, which were believed to lead to the eventual creation of panels that would confer on whether or not patients should be allowed to seek health care or be chosen to die as a result of their illness.

Reference

Rutenberg, J., & Calmes, J. (2009, August 13). False 'death panel' rumor has some familiar roots. *The New York Times Online*. Retrieved from http://www.nytimes.com/2009/08/14/health/policy/14panel.html

Debt ceiling The debt ceiling is the maximum amount of debt that a government can take on. In order to spend past this ceiling, Congress must agree to raise it.

Reference

Goldstein, J. (2011, April 11). The debt ceiling explained. *NPR: Planet Money* [Web log]. Retrieved from http://www.npr.org/blogs/money/2011/04/12/135314575/the-debt-ceiling-explained

Defense of Marriage Act (DOMA) DOMA is a federal statute enacted under President Bill Clinton in 1996. It provides that no state can be required to recognize or give effect to same-sex marriages. It defines the term "marriage" for purposes of federal law as the union of a man and a woman as husband and wife, and defines "spouse" for purposes of federal law as being only a person of the opposite sex. DOMA was enacted in response to the fear that if one state sanctioned or permitted same-sex marriages, other states would also have to give full faith and credit to such marriages.

Reference

US Legal Inc. (2012). *Defense of Marriage Act Law & legal definition. Definitions.* Retrieved from http://definitions.uslegal.com/d/defense-of-marriage-act/

Did you know...

Colgate faced a big obstacle marketing toothpaste in Spanish-speaking countries. Colgate translates into the command, "Go hang yourself."
Great Facts.com: http://www.greatfacts.com/

Delegate See **State delegate**.

Department of Agriculture (USDA) This cabinet department has a broad range of responsibilities that include farming and agricultural products, food stamps and antipoverty programs, and conservation and natural resource protection. Agriculture department inspectors are responsible for the safety of the nation's food supply and USDA employees run various rural development programs. The U.S. Forest Service, which include park rangers and firefighters, is a USDA agency.

Reference

Partnership for Public Service. (n.d.). *Cabinet departments and what they do*. Retrieved from http://www.makingthedifference.org/federalcareers/cabinetdepartments.shtml

Department of Commerce This cabinet department is responsible for everything we buy and sell. Commerce officials regulate everything from foreign trade to fishing to the granting of patents. The department also oversees programs that support minority businesses, and provides statistics and analyses for business and government planners.

Reference

Partnership for Public Service. (n.d.). *Cabinet departments and what they do*. Retrieved from http://www.makingthedifference.org/federalcareers/cabinetdepartments.shtml

Department of Defense This cabinet is responsible for supplying military hardware, administering military pay and benefits to its personnel, disseminating pertinent information to the public and the military, creating and implementing military-based educational programs, and locating prisoners of war and missing military personnel.

Reference

Partnership for Public Service. (n.d.). *Cabinet departments and what they do*. Retrieved from http://www.makingthedifference.org/federalcareers/cabinetdepartments.shtml

Department of Education This cabinet department is responsible for helping to supply institutions of learning with resources and supplies, qualified teachers, national standards, and emerging technology for the classroom.

Reference

Partnership for Public Service. (n.d.). *Cabinet departments and what they do*. Retrieved from http://www.makingthedifference.org/federalcareers/ cabinetdepartments.shtml

Department of Energy This cabinet department works to ensure that the country has a consistent, reliable, and safe supply of energy. This energy can be harnessed in the form of nuclear energy, energy from fossil fuels, or from green sources, such as solar energy and wind energy.

Reference

Partnership for Public Service. (n.d.). *Cabinet departments and what they do*. Retrieved from http://www.makingthedifference.org/federalcareers/ cabinetdepartments.shtml

Did you know...

China has more English speakers than the United States.
Great Facts.com: http://www.greatfacts.com/

Department of Health and Human Services (HHS) This cabinet department is responsible for overseeing the health and well-being of the American people. HHS employees work on more than 300 programs and perform essential services ranging from food safety to medical research to drug abuse prevention.

Reference

Partnership for Public Service. (n.d.). *Cabinet departments and what they do*. Retrieved from http://www.makingthedifference.org/federalcareers/ cabinetdepartments.shtml

Department of Homeland Security This cabinet department's first priority is to protect the nation from further terrorist attacks, along with securing the nation's borders, analyzing and interpreting threats from abroad, protecting the nation's airports and critical infrastructure, and coordinating the nation's response to threats from outside entities.

Reference

Partnership for Public Service. (n.d.). *Cabinet departments and what they do*. Retrieved from http://www.makingthedifference.org/federalcareers/ cabinetdepartments.shtml

Department of Housing and Urban Development This cabinet department is primarily responsible for ensuring that America's families have access to safe, affordable, and decent housing. One of its most important roles is insuring mortgages and loans for home buyers and providing loans for home improvements for existing homes. The department is also responsible for giving direct loans for construction or rehabilitation of housing projects for the elderly and the handicapped, providing federal housing subsidies for low- and moderate-income families, and enforcing fair housing and equal housing access laws.

Reference

Partnership for Public Service. (n.d.). *Cabinet departments and what they do*. Retrieved from http://www.makingthedifference.org/federalcareers/ cabinetdepartments.shtml

Department of Interior This cabinet department manages the nation's natural resources, from land and water to coal and natural gas. By monitoring the extraction of natural resources, Interior Department personnel work to protect and preserve the environment. This department also houses the office responsible for overseeing Native American affairs.

Reference

Partnership for Public Service. (n.d.). *Cabinet departments and what they do*. Retrieved from http://www.makingthedifference.org/federalcareers/ cabinetdepartments.shtml

Department of Justice This cabinet department is headed by the attorney general, and is charged with implementing and enforcing federal laws which aim to protect the public and maintain fair business practices. The FBI is housed within this department, and immigration and naturalization matters are dealt with, as well.

Reference

> Partnership for Public Service. (n.d.). *Cabinet departments and what they do*. Retrieved from http://www.makingthedifference.org/federalcareers/cabinetdepartments.shtml

Department of Labor This cabinet department is responsible for administering and enforcing laws that ensure safe working environments for workers, including minimum wages and overtime. This department also ensures the rights of and the work conditions for the disabled, the elderly, and minorities. The department maintains job banks, unemployment benefits, and healthy workplace standards.

Reference

> Partnership for Public Service. (n.d.). *Cabinet departments and what they do*. Retrieved from http://www.makingthedifference.org/federalcareers/cabinetdepartments.shtml

Department of State The head of this department is the secretary of state. The department is responsible primarily with forming and maintaining diplomatic relationships with other nations. The department communicates the foreign policy of the United States and helps to develop policy that represents those aims to the world, abroad. The department negotiates treaties with foreign governments and helps to ensure the safety of citizens of the nation who travel abroad.

Reference

> Partnership for Public Service. (n.d.). *Cabinet departments and what they do*. Retrieved from http://www.makingthedifference.org/federalcareers/cabinetdepartments.shtml

Department of Transportation This cabinet department is responsible for the roads, bridges, highways, and other transportation infrastructure located within the borders of the country. Cars, trucks, trains, subways, airplanes, and all vehicles of transport, are regulated under this department.

Reference

> Partnership for Public Service. (n.d.). *Cabinet departments and what they do*. Retrieved from http://www.makingthedifference.org/federalcareers/cabinetdepartments.shtml

Department of Treasury This cabinet department is responsible for many of the financial aspects of the government. Printing the nation's money is only one of many responsibilities overseen by this second oldest cabinet department (only the State Department has been around longer). The department also sets domestic financial, economic, and tax policy; manages the public debt; and collects taxes. A lesser known role of this department is law enforcement; it houses both Secret Service and the Customs Service agencies.

Reference

> Partnership for Public Service. (n.d.). *Cabinet departments and what they do*. Retrieved from http://www.makingthedifference.org/federalcareers/cabinetdepartments.shtml

Department of Veterans Affairs This cabinet department is primarily responsible for ensuring the safety, security, and smooth transition back into civilian life for the nation's veterans. The department regulates veteran work programs and veterans hospitals, promotes the hiring of veterans, and supplies veteran pension programs.

Reference

> Partnership for Public Service. (n.d.). *Cabinet departments and what they do*. Retrieved from http://www.makingthedifference.org/federalcareers/cabinetdepartments.shtml

Dog-whistle politics A colloquial term used in reference to political speech or political rhetoric that employs coded language to mean one thing to the general population but has a different or more specific meaning for a targeted subgroup of the audience.

Reference

Dog-whistle politics. (2012). In *Taegan Goddard's political dictionary*. Retrieved from http://politicaldictionary.com/words/dog-whistle-politics/

Don't Ask, Don't Tell (DADT) A policy passed by Congress in 1993 while President Bill Clinton was in office, and later signed by him. This policy denies openly homosexual persons the right to serve in the military. The policy was overturned under President Barack Obama, who signed the repeal into law effective September 20, 2011.

Reference

Servicemembers Legal Defense Network. (2012). *About "Don't Ask, Don't Tell."* Retrieved from http://www.sldn.org/pages/about-dadt

Do-Nothing Congress Pejorative term originally used in reference to the 80th Congress, and refers to its failure to engage in debate and/or pass legislation. The term has most recently been used in reference to the 111th-112th Congress.

Reference

Silverleib, A. (2011). *Obama, Truman, and the "do-nothing" Congress*. CNN online. Retrieved from http://articles.cnn.com/2011-12-27/politics/politics_obama-do-nothing-congress_1_debt-ceiling-debate-house-speaker-john-boehner-trillion-in-deficit-reduction?_s=PM:POLITICS

Did you know...

On average, 749 pounds of paper products are used by an American individual annually. Great Facts.com: http://www.greatfacts.com/

E

Electoral college It consists of the electors appointed by each state who formally elect the president and vice president of the United States. Since 1964, there have been 538 electors in each presidential election. This provision is detailed in Article II, Section 1, Clause 2 of the United States Constitution. See also **State delegate.**

Reference

> Electoral College. (2011). In *Oxford advanced learner's dictionary online*. Retrieved from http://oald8.oxfordlearnersdictionaries.com/dictionary/electoral-college

Endorsement To approve openly, especially to express support or approval of a political candidate.

Reference

> Endorsement. (2006). In *Merriam-Webster's collegiate dictionary* (11th ed.). Springfield, MA: Merriam-Webster Inc.

> *Did you know...*
>
> Franklin Pierce was the first U.S. president to have a Christmas tree in the White House. Great Facts.com: http://www.greatfacts.com/

Enemy combatant A term first used by President Franklin D. Roosevelt, in the early 1940s, which was used to refer to citizens who associate themselves with the military arm of an enemy government. With its aid, guidance, and direction, these individuals enter the United States to commit hostile acts.

Most recently, the term was employed by President George W. Bush in the aftermath of September 11, 2001, to refer to unlawful combatants not related to a military outfit. Once determined by the president to be an enemy combatant, persons may be held indefinitely and are subject to the jurisdiction of military tribunals. Captured enemy combatants, whether soldiers or saboteurs, may be detained for the duration of hostilities. They need not be "guilty" of anything; they are detained simply by virtue of their status as enemy combatants in war.

On March 13, 2009, U.S. Attorney General Eric Holder issued a statement that the United States had abandoned the Bush administration's term, enemy combatant.

References

Gonzales, A.R. (2004 , February 24). *Remarks before the American Bar Association Standing Committee on Law and National Security*. Retrieved from http://www.fas.org/irp/news/2004/02/gonzales.pdf

Haynes II, W.J. (2002, December 12). *Enemy combatants*. Council on Foreign Relations. Retrieved from http://www.cfr.org/international-law/enemy-combatants/p5312

Entitlement program A kind of government program that provides individuals with personal financial benefits to which an indefinite number of potential beneficiaries have a legal right whenever they meet eligibility conditions that are specified by the standing law that authorizes the program. Common examples of these programs include Social Security, Medicare, and Medicaid.

References

Johnson, P.M. (2005). *A glossary of political economy terms*. Auburn, AL: Department of Political Science, Auburn University. Retrieved from http://www.auburn.edu/~johnspm/gloss/entitlement_program

Entrance poll An informal poll of voters, which collects information about the voters' intentions, demographics, and the voters' general policy interests and positions. Similar to exit polls but conducted on entry into the polling location, these polls are often used to predict the outcome of an election, and to gather demographic data about the electorate.

Reference

Entrance poll. (n.d.). In *Merriam-Webster online dictionary* (11th ed.). Retrieved from http://www.merriam-webster.com/dictionary/exit%20poll

Did you know...

Women are twice as likely to be diagnosed with depression as men in the United States. Great Facts.com: http://www.greatfacts.com/

Executive branch One of the three branches of government. It consists of the president and cabinet members.

Reference

> The White House. (2012). *Executive branch. Our government.* Retrieved from http://www.whitehouse.gov/our-government/executive-branch

Exit poll An informal poll of voters on their way out of a polling location, which collects information about the voters' electoral choices while in the booth, demographics, and the voters' general policy interests and positions. These polls are often used to predict the outcome of an election, and to gather demographic data about the electorate.

Reference

> Exit poll. (n.d.). In *Merriam-Webster online dictionary* (11th ed.). Retrieved from http://www.merriam-webster.com/dictionary/exit%20poll

Facebook© A social networking website that allows individuals and organizations to create profiles to share information (e.g., events, life status, thoughts, and pictures) with a user-selected subgroup of approved Facebook users called "friends." Facebook has become a powerful social tool for garnering and leveraging the power of community for social, political, and corporate benefit. Facebook was founded in 2004 by Harvard student Mark Zuckerberg; it was originally called "thefacebook."

Reference

> Rayport, J. (2011, February 2). What is facebook, really? *Harvard Business Review Online.* Retrieved from http://blogs.hbr.org/cs/2011/02/what_is_facebook_is_becoming.html

Filibuster A type of parliamentary procedure. Specifically, it is the right of an individual to extend debate, allowing a lone member to delay or entirely prevent a vote on a given proposal. It is commonly referred to as talking out a bill, and is characterized as a form of obstruction in a legislature or other decision-making body. The term in its legislative sense was first used in 1854 when opponents tried to delay the Kansas-Nebraska Act in the U.S. Congress.

Reference

Filibuster. (n.d.). In *United States Senate glossary online* Retrieved from http://www.senate.gov/reference/glossary_term/filibuster.htm

Flat tax This tax is an income tax system in which everyone pays the same tax rate regardless of their income. Flat tax systems are in place in several U.S. states. This tax reform policy has also been proposed by candidates for national elected office.

Reference

Investopedia. (2012). *Flat tax*. Retrieved from http://www.investopedia.com/terms/f/flattax.asp#axzz1wViYhub0

Did you know...

The national anthem of Greece has 158 verses.
Great Facts.com: http://www.greatfacts.com/

Flip-flop A derogatory term used to refer to a political candidate who has been cited as holding opposing opinions on one issue or another. This is usually characterized by a sudden change of position on a policy, strategy, or issue.

Reference

Flip-flop. (2006). *Merriam-Webster's collegiate dictionary* (11th ed.). Springfield, MA: Merriam-Webster.

Did you know...

Annually, Americans eat 45 million turkeys at Thanksgiving.
Great Facts.com: http://www.greatfacts.com/

G

Gerrymandering The act of manipulating the boundaries of an electoral constituency so as to favor one party or class. This term was first used in the 19th century and was named after Governor Elbridge Gerry of Massachusetts and a salamander, from the supposed similarity between a salamander and the shape of a new voting district on a map drawn when he was in office (1812).

Reference

Gerrymander. (2012). In *Oxford dictionaries online*. Retrieved from http://oxforddictionaries.com/definition/gerrymander

Gitmo (GTMO) Refers to Guantanamo Bay, the site of a U.S. naval base in Guantanamo, Cuba. Guantanamo is a city located in southeastern Cuba. In this U.S. military detention facility, prisoners are held in seven different detention camps. Since 2002, 779 prisoners have been held at Guantanamo Bay, with 171 remaining as of March 2012. According to camp records, 600 prisoners have been released and 8 have died at the facility since it began to be used as a military prison in 2002. Prior to the use of Guantanamo Bay as a military prison, it was used to detain refugees from countries such as Cuba and Haiti.

References

Guantanamo. (n.d.). In *The free dictionary online*. Retrieved from http://www.thefreedictionary.com/Guantanamo

Guantanamo Bay [GTMO]. (2011, May 7). *GITMO*. Retrieved May 28, 2012 from http://www.globalsecurity.org/military/facility/guantanamo-bay.htm

GOP (Grand Old Party) A term used to refer to the Republican party. First used in 1924 as a result of a cartoon by legendary political cartoonist Thomas Nast, who in an 1874 issue of *Harper's Weekly*, depicted the Democrats as a donkey trying to scare a Republican elephant. Originally meaning the Gallant Old Party, the common acronym has evolved to mean the Grand Old Party.

Reference

Grace, F. (2009, February 11). *What does GOP stand for?* CBS News online. Retrieved from http://www.cbsnews.com/2100-250_162-531460.html

House majority leader A senior member of the U.S. House of Representatives who has been chosen to lead the caucus. This leader is responsible for scheduling legislation for floor consideration; planning the daily, weekly, and annual legislative agendas; consulting with members to gauge the party; and, in general, working to advance the goals of the majority party. This member is ranked below the Speaker of the House.

Reference

United States House of Representatives. (2012). Majority and minority leaders. *House History*. Retrieved from http://artandhistory.house.gov/house_history/leaders.aspx

House majority whip A member of the majority party in the U.S. House of Representatives who is charged with assisting the house majority leader in assessing and counting the number of members of the party's caucus who can be expected to support a measure to be debated on the floor. The term whip comes from a fox-hunting expression ("whipper-in"), referring to the member of the hunting team responsible for keeping the dogs from straying from the team during a chase.

Reference

United States House of Representatives. (2012). Majority and minority leaders. *House History*. Retrieved from http://artandhistory.house.gov/house_history/leaders.aspx

Did you know...

The concept of Boxing Day, which is on December 26th, was to give boxes of food and clothing to the poor. It is now viewed in some countries as a time to get merchandise from stores at reduced prices.
Great Facts.com: http://www.greatfacts.com/

House minority leader A member of the U.S. House of Representatives who is chosen to lead the members of the minority party caucus (also called the "loyal opposition"). This leader works in a similar manner to the majority leader with the distinct goal of protecting the minority's rights and interests.

Reference

United States House of Representatives. (2012). Majority and minority leaders. *House History.* Retrieved from http://artandhistory.house.gov/house_history/leaders.aspx

House minority whip A member of the minority party in the U.S. House of Representatives who is charged with assisting the house minority leader in assessing and counting the number of members of the minority caucus who can be expected to vote in support of a measure to be debated on the House floor. The term whip comes from a fox-hunting expression ("whipper-in"), referring to the member of the hunting team responsible for keeping the dogs from straying from the team during a chase.

Reference

United States House of Representatives. (2012). Majority and minority leaders. *House History.* Retrieved from http://artandhistory.house.gov/house_history/leaders.aspx

I

Incumbent (noun) The candidate in an electoral race who currently holds the seat being sought.

Reference

Incumbent. (2006). In *Merriam-Webster's collegiate dictionary* (11th ed.). Springfield, MA: Merriam-Webster

Did you know...

Black pepper is the most popular spice in the world.
Great Facts.com: http://www.greatfacts.com/

Incumbency effect The perceived and/or quantifiable advantages and disadvantages a candidate for office experiences as a result of being the incumbent candidate in the race.

Numerous studies show that beginning in the 1960s incumbents were able to win more frequently and increase their vote percentages. Incumbents have always had a high success rate versus challengers, and now they do even better.

Reference

Stonecash, J. (2008). *Reassessing the incumbency effect*. New York: Cambridge.

Insurgency Insurgency is a movement, a political effort with a specific aim. This sets it apart from guerrilla warfare and terrorism, as they are both methods available to pursue the goals of the political movement. The ultimate goal of an insurgency is to challenge the existing government for control of all or a portion of its territory, or force political concessions in sharing political power.

Reference

Differences between Terrorism and Insurgency. (n.d.). *Terrorism research*. Retrieved from http://www.terrorism-research.com/insurgency/

Interest group A group of participants who organize and take action in an effort to effect legislative or institutional policy change regarding a particular topic of collective interest. These also called special interest groups.

Reference

Interest Group. (2012). In *Encyclopedia Britannica online*. Retrieved from http://www.britannica.com/EBchecked/topic/290136/interest-group

Did you know...

Close to 73% of girls in Bangladesh are married by age 18.
Great Facts.com: http://www.greatfacts.com/

Iron-triangle An interconnected relationship among three political actors (the legislature, interest groups, and bureaucracies) whose actions effect one another and whose relationship is relatively interdependent.

Reference

Johnson, P.M. (2005). *Iron triangles. A glossary of political economy terms.* Retrieved from http://www.britannica.com/EBchecked/topic/290136/interest-group

Judicial branch The branch of the federal government made up of the Supreme Court and other federal courts.

Reference

The White House. (2012). *The judicial branch.* Retrieved from http://www.whitehouse.gov/our-government/judicial-branch

K Street The downtown Washington, D.C., avenue where many lobbyists and lawyers have offices.

Reference

Congressman Charles B. Rangel. (2012). *K Street. Glossary.* http://rangel.house.gov/legislation/glossary.shtml#K

Legislative branch One of the three branches of government. It consists of the U.S. Senate and the U.S. House of Representatives. Often referred to as the law-making branch of the U.S. government.

Reference

The White House. (2012). *Legislative branch. Our government.* Retrieved from http://www.whitehouse.gov/our-government/legislative-branch

Liberal A political ideology which espouses the need for government action in an effort to achieve equal opportunity and equal access to resources. Liberals typically believe that it is the duty of government to alleviate social ills and to protect civil liberties, individual rights, and human rights.

Reference

Conservative vs. Liberal Beliefs. (2010). Retrieved May 28, 2012 from
    http://www.studentnewsdaily.com/conservative-vs.-liberal-beliefs/

Libertarian A member of a political party advocating libertarian principles. Libertarians strongly oppose any government interfering in their personal, family, and business decisions. Libertarians believe in, and pursue, personal freedom while maintaining personal responsibility. The Libertarian party itself serves a much larger proliberty community with the specific mission of electing Libertarians to public office.

Reference

Libertarian Party. (2012). *FAQ: What is a libertarian?* Retrieved from
    http://www.lp.org/faq

Lobby A group that attempts to influence a legislation or government spending plans to achieve an outcome more favorable to its agenda or objectives.

Reference

Lobby. (n.d.). In *The business dictionary*. Retrieved from
    http://www.businessdictionary.com/definition/lobby.html

Log-cabin republican An interest which aligns itself with many of the core values of the GOP, while advocating for the freedom and equality of gay and lesbian Americans.

Reference

Log Cabin Republicans. (2012). *About Log Cabin Republicans*. Retrieved on May 28,
    2012 from http://www.logcabin.org/site/c.nsKSL7PMLpF/b.5466967/k.C986/
    About_Us.htm

Margin of error The amount of discrepancy in a statistical measure that can be attributed to statistical error or some other miscalculation.

Reference

George Mason University. (n.d.). *What is the margin of error in a poll?* Statistical Assessment Service. Retrieved from http://stats.org/in_depth/faq/margin_of_error.htm

Medicaid A joint federal and state health care program designed to provide low or no-cost health care insurance coverage for some people with limited income and resources.

Reference

U.S. Department of Health and Human Services. (2012). *Glossary: Medicaid.* Retrieved from http://www.medicare.gov/Glossary/m.html

Medicare A federally-funded health care program designed to provide low- or no-cost health care insurance coverage for the elderly (over 65 years of age) and younger disabled people, and people with end-stage renal disease (permanent kidney failure requiring dialysis or a transplant).

Reference

U.S. Department of Health and Human Services. (2012). *Glossary: Medicare.* Retrieved from http://www.medicare.gov/Glossary/m.html

Mid-term election Elections for national political office which are held in the years between U.S. presidential elections.

References

Washington Post. (n.d.). *Midterm election. Politics: Glossary.* Retrieved from http://projects.washingtonpost.com/politicsglossary/election/midterm-election/

Abramowitz, A., & Ornstein, N. (2010, August 15). Five myths about midterm elections. *The Washington Post.* Retrieved from http://www.washingtonpost.com/wp-dyn/content/article/2010/08/12/AR2010081203591.html

Mobilization (voter) Measures taken in an effort to help or motivate voters to get to the polls and cast a vote for their preferred candidate for political office. These efforts can take the form of registration drives, aid with transportation to and from the polls, educating potential voters, and volunteering at a local precinct. Candidates and their campaigns often times engage in numerous mobilization efforts in order to increase the likelihood of favorable voter participation on day.

References

Darlington & Darlington, 2012.

Green, D. (n.d.). The science (and pseudoscience) of winning elections. [Powerpoint slides]. Retrieved from https://docs.google.com/viewer?a=v&q=cache:59YTEtF QosQJ:vote.research.yale.edu/The%2520Science%2520and%2520Pseudoscienc e%2520of%2520Winning%2520Elections%2520--%2520Fall%25202008.ppt+v oter+mobilization+definition&hl=en&gl=us&pid=bl&srcid=ADGEESjgPF0dV 8Q3FZjMGS8vNDafhXDpppa30Pf-6Aa8SBwVeLxm5Ziu3MEhx07Ue9CL-BzN9XlPhHBB4Mu-fWrZHrhYDpe4hKKwB-O6dgyFK_zQXlIPK8AlPt_ ioGnKecLwpWsW7-Fb&sig=AHIEtbQFl5Xk28X9CQwgc45-EC_Lb7rJOQ

Negative campaigning A campaign effort which centers its message on highlighting the negative aspects of an opponent's policy positions and/or personal attributes in an effort to discredit that opponent.

Reference

Darlington & Darlington, 2012.

NIMBY (Not in my back yard) A colloquial term used to refer to positions which support that a particular public policy action be taken, as long as the lasting effects are "not [present] 'in my backyard.'" In other words, as long as the proponents of a particular policy position can be shielded from the negative repercussions of that policy position, support can and will be garnered.

References

NIMBY. (2006). In *Merriam-Webster's collegiate dictionary* (11th ed.). Springfield, MA: Merriam-Webster.

NIMBY. (n.d.). Definitions.net. Retrieved May 28, 2012 from http://www.definitions.net/definition/NIMBY

Did you know...

There are more than 40 million Americans who have "chronic halitosis," which is bad breath that never goes away. Great Facts.com: http://www.greatfacts.com/

O

Obamacare A term, usually used disparagingly, to refer to the Patient Protection and Affordable Care Act, passed under President Barack Obama and enacted in 2010.

Reference

Cox, A., Desantis, A., Parlapiano, A., & White, J. (2012, March 25). Fighting to control the meaning of "Obamacare." *The New York Times*. Retrieved from http://www.nytimes.com/interactive/2012/03/25/us/politics/fighting-to-control-the-meaning-of-obamacare.html

Obamneycare A term, usually used disparagingly, to refer to the Patient Protection and Affordable Care Act, passed under President Barack Obama and enacted in 2010. This term specifically makes further reference to the similarities between the Affordable Care Act and legislation passed by Governor Willard "Mitt" Romney during his tenure as governor of Massachusetts.

Reference

Vogel, K. (June 11, 2011). Pawlenty pans "Obamaneycare." *Politico*. Retrieved from http://www.politico.com/blogs/politicolive/0611/Pawlenty_pans_ Obamney_care.html

> *Did you know...*
>
> The country with the highest consumption of candy, at 29.5 pounds annually per person, is Denmark. Great Facts.com: http://www.greatfacts.com/

Occupy Wall Street A grassroots, people-oriented movement that began on September 17, 2011, in New York City. The movement, which aimed at exposing and changing the common practices of Wall Street banks and other institutions that are believed to operate at the expense of the middle-class in American society, spread to more than 100 cities worldwide.

Reference

OccupyWallStreet. (n.d.) About. Retrieved May 28, 2012 from http://occupywallst. org/about/

Open primary A direct primary election which allows eligible voters, regardless of the party to which they are registered, to vote for candidates running for primary election.

Reference

Dictionary.com. (n.d.). *Open primary*. Retrieved from http://dictionary.reference.com/browse/open+primary?qsrc=2446

P

PAC (political action committee) A political action committee (PAC) is any organization in the United States that campaigns for or against political candidates, ballot initiatives, or legislation. According to the Federal Election Campaign Act, an organization becomes a PAC when it receives or spends more than $1,000 for the purpose of influencing a federal election. At the state level, an organization becomes a PAC when it meets the state's specific election laws.

Candidates and traditional candidate committees can accept $2,500 from individuals, per election. However, candidates and traditional candidate committees are prohibited from accepting money from corporations, unions, and associations. Additionally, federal election code prohibits those entities from contributing directly to candidates or candidate committees.

References

Federal Election Commission. (2008). *Federal campaign finance laws*. Retrieved from http://www.fec.gov/law/feca/feca.pdf

Kentucky: Secretary of State. (2010). *Civics glossary*. Retrieved from http://www.sos.ky.gov/kids/civics/glossary.htm

Partisan A position on a political matter which solely favors or supports one particular ideology or party over another.

Reference

Partisan. (2006). In *Merriam-Webster's collegiate dictionary* (11th ed.). Springfield, MA: Merriam-Webster.

Party of "no" A term, usually used disparagingly, which refers to the Republicans in Congress (especially during the 111th and 112th Congress), which references their tendency to vote against many pieces of legislation sponsored by members of the Democratic party in Congress and/or President Obama.

Reference

Darlington & Darlington 2012.

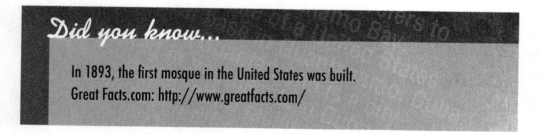

Did you know...

In 1893, the first mosque in the United States was built.
Great Facts.com: http://www.greatfacts.com/

Party platform An oftentimes written expression of the positions a political party takes on certain issues concerning public interest. These positions usually communicate the overall ideological stance of party members and candidates who run for election as representatives of a given party.

Reference

> The American Presidency Project. (n.d.). Retrieved from http://www.presidency.ucsb.edu/index.php

Party politics Policy creation and political maneuvering that is said to benefit the interests of a political party structure over the interests of the public, as a whole.

Reference

> Dictionary.com. (n.d). *Party politics*. Retrieved from http://dictionary.reference.com/browse/party+politics?qsrc=2446

PIPA (Protect Intellectual Privacy Act) Official name: Preventing Real Online Threats to Economic Creativity and Theft of Intellectual Property Act. Introduced May 12, 2011 by Senator Patrick Leahy (D-VT) with bipartisan support. This act was put into place as a measure to curb access to rogue websites dedicated to facilitating copyright infringement, circumventing technology that controls access to copyrighted works, or selling or promoting counterfeit goods or services, especially those registered outside of the United States.

Reference

> Govtrack.us. http://www.govtrack.us/congress/bills/112/s968

Pocketbook voting The tendency for a voter to vote for a candidate based on his or her position on policies that may affect that voter's personal economic condition.

Reference

Elinder, M., Jordahl, H., & Poutvaara, P. (2008). Selfish and prospective: Theory and evidence of pocketbook voting. Retrieved from http://ftp.iza.org/dp3763.pdf

Poison pill amendment Term used to refer to a piece of legislation written into a larger piece of legislation, which is considered so distasteful and unlikely to be supported, that its inclusion is likely to cause the entire measure to fail passage.

Reference

Poison Pill Amendment. (2012). In *The Oxford Dictionaries online*. Retrieved from http://oxforddictionaries.com/definition/poison+pill+amendment?region=us

Political football A policy issue or a politically salient event that is rhetorically used to garner political support or to gain favorable political positioning among voters.

Reference

The Free Online Dictionary. (n.d.). *Idioms and phrases*. http://idioms.thefreedictionary.com/a+political+football

Political insider A term, usually with negative connotation, used to refer to a politician or political actor, who has spent a considerable portion of his or her career navigating the political arena, especially in Washington, D.C.

Reference

Darlington & Darlington, 2012.

Political outsider A political actor who has not centered his or her career around politics, and is usually not associated with Washington, D.C., politics.

Reference

Darlington & Darlington, 2012.

Political party A political organization that consists of constituents, representatives, and elected officials who aim to influence policy and who typically have a similar ideology concerning certain issues, and typically converge on ways in which to approach a given policy issue. Political parties engage in electoral campaign, protests, and educational outreach efforts, in an effort to communicate an ideology, which is often written out as a party platform.

Reference

Dictionary.com. http://dictionary.reference.com/browse/party+politics?qsrc=2446

Pop culture The shorter and colloquial term for referring to the popular culture of a society normally disseminated through mass media (e.g., television).

Reference

Pop. (2006). In *Merriam-Webster's collegiate dictionary* (11th ed.). Springfield, MA: Merriam-Webster.

Primary An election held in the early part of the electoral process which is designed to narrow down the field of candidates within a political party, to then go on to run against a candidate from an opposing party in a general election.

Reference

Dictionary.com. (n.d.). Primary. Retrieved from http://dictionary.reference.com/browse/primary

Pro-choice An ideology that supports the right of women to seek safe and accessible abortion services and other reproductive health services and supports the U.S. Supreme Court decision in *Roe v. Wade.*

Reference

Pro choice American. (n.d.). http://www.naral.org/

Progressivism Progressivism is a general political philosophy that advocates or favors social, political, and economic reform or changes usually in opposition to conservative or reactionary ideologies. It emerged as part of a more general response to the cast changes brought by industrialization and as an alternative to the traditional conservative response to social and economic issues.

Reference

Nugent, W. (2010). *Progressivism: A very short introduction.* New York: Oxford University Press.

Pro-life The term pro-life was coined by U.S. leaders of the right-to-life (antiabortion) movement following the January 1973 U.S. Supreme Court case *Roe vs. Wade.* The term pro-life was adopted instead of antiabortion to highlight the belief that they consider abortion the taking of a human life, rather than an issue concerning the restriction of women's reproductive rights.

Reference

Schultz, J.D., & Van Assendelft, L.A. (1999). *The American political landscape series: Encyclopedia of women in American politics.* Phoenix, AZ: The Oryx Press.

Proportional delegate allocation An electoral system that awards candidates a number of delegates based on the proportion of the vote received in a given election.

Reference

FairVote, The Center for Voting and Democracy. (2012). *Delegate allocation rules in 2012 GOP nomination race: The spectrum from proportional representation to winner take all*. Retrieved from http://www.fairvote.org/delegate-allocation-rules-in-2012-gop

Public option Refers to the government-run health insurance plan proposed in the U.S. House of Representative's health care bill in 2009 (America's Affordable Health Choices Act of 2009), that would compete alongside private insurers in a health insurance exchange set up by the legislation.

References

The Patient Protection and Affordable Care Act Detailed Summary Retrieved from http://dpc.senate.gov/healthreformbill/healthbill04. pdf.
"Examining the public option in healthcare reform".(September 1, 2009). PBS Newhour. Retrieved from http://www.pbs.org/newshour/bb/health/july-dec09/health_09-01.html.

R

Race-baiting A term used to refer to the use of a particularly salient political issue in such a way that racial elements are exploited, and racial sensitivity is agitated.

Reference

Darlington & Darlington, 2012.

Rational choice theory A principle of criminology which posits that man is a rational actor who weighs the costs and benefits, ways and means of a given choice, and will make the choice that benefits him the most, at the least cost.

Reference

US Legal. (n.d.). *Rational choice theory [Criminology] law and legal definition*. Retrieved from http://definitions.uslegal.com/r/rational-choice-theory-criminology/

Reagan Democrat Traditionally Democratic voters who were drawn to Ronald Reagan in the early 1980s for his ideology of social conservatism and fiscal responsibility.

Reference

Regan-Democrat. (n.d.). *The Washington Post*. Retrieved from http://projects.washingtonpost.com/politicsglossary/party-affiliated/Reagan-Democrat/

Re-call election A procedure that allows citizens to remove and replace a public official before the end of a term of office. Recall is a political process unlike impeachment which is the legal procedure to remove an elected official.

Reference

National Council of State Legislatures. (2012, May 8). *Recall of state officials*. Retrieved from http://www.ncsl.org/legislatures-elections/elections/recall-of-state-officials.aspx#Constitutions

Recession A term meaning a period of reduced economic activity. In 2008, this term gained significance as a means of characterizing the drastic downturn which began toward the end of the Bush presidency. This economic period has often been referred to as "the worst recession since the Great Depression."

Reference

Recession. (2006). In *Merriam-Webster's collegiate dictionary* (11th ed.). Springfield, MA: Merriam-Webster.

Did you know...

Senator Margaret Chase Smith (ME) was the first woman to be placed in nomination for president at a major party convention, when Senator George Aiken nominated her at the 1964 Republican national convention. Smith was also the first woman to serve in both the House and the Senate.
Center for American Women and Politics: http://www.cawp.rutgers.edu/fast_facts/resources/Didyouknow.php#pres

Referendum A policy item that is put on the ballot for the electorate to vote on, as opposed to the typical legislative process most laws undergo.

Reference

> Referendum. (n.d.). In *Merriam-Webster online dictionary* (11th ed.). Retrieved from http://www.merriam-webster.com/dictionary/referendum

RINO (Republican-in-name-only) An oftentimes derogatory term used to denote a person who classifies oneself as a Republican, but whose actions and voting record do not typically fall in line with the ideology of the party.

Reference

> Darlington & Darlington, 2012).

Run-off election A final election to decide an earlier election that has not resulted in a decision in favor of any one candidate.

Reference

> Run-off. (2006). In *Merriam-Webster's collegiate dictionary* (11th ed.). Springfield, MA: Merriam-Webster.

Did you know...

In 1972, Representative Shirley Chisholm (D-NY) ran for president of the United States, in the Democratic primaries. At the party's national convention, she was awarded 151.25 delegate votes before Senator George McGovern won the nomination.
Center for American Women and Politics: http://www.cawp.rutgers.edu/fast_facts/resources/Didyouknow.php#pres

Senate majority leader A senior member of the majority party in the Senate who has been elected by the party conference to serve as the chief Senate spokesperson for the party. This person also manages and schedules the legislative and executive business of the Senate and usually has priority as floor leader in being "recognized to speak" on the Senate floor.

References

United States Senate. (n.d.). *Glossary: Floor leaders*. Retrieved from
http://www.senate.gov/reference/glossary_term/floor_leaders.htm
United States Senate. (n.d.). *Party leadership: Majority and minority leaders and party whips*. Retrieved from http://www.senate.gov/artandhistory/history/common/briefing/Majority Minority_Leaders.htm

Senate minority leader A senior member of the minority party in the Senate who has been elected by the party conference to serve as the chief Senate spokesperson for the party. This person also manages and schedules the legislative and executive business of the Senate and usually has similar priority as majority leader in being "recognized to speak" on the Senate floor.

References

Floor leaders. (n.d.). In *Glossary, United States Senate.* [Web] Retrieved from
http://www.senate.gov/reference/glossary_term/floor_leaders.htm
United States Senate. (n.d.). *Party leadership: Majority and minority leaders and party whips*. Retrieved from http://www.senate.gov/artandhistory/history/common/briefing/Majority_Minority_Leaders.htm

Did you know...

Geraldine A. Ferraro (D-NY), a third-term congresswoman and Secretary of the House Democratic Caucus, became the first woman to run on a major party's national ticket, when she was selected by Walter F. Mondale as his vice presidential running mate (1984).
Center for American Women and Politics: http://www.cawp.rutgers.edu/fast_facts/resources/Didyouknow.php#pres

Senate whips These assistants to their party's Senate floor leader (either majority or minority) mobilize votes within their parties on major issues. In the absence of their respective party floor leader, the whip often serves as acting floor leader.

Reference

> Whips. (n.d.). In *Glossary, United States Senate* [Web]. Retrieved from http://www.senate.gov/reference/glossary_term/whips.htm

Signing statement A provision afforded to the president of the United States, which allows the president to sign a bill into law with the addition of specific conditions that are stipulated in the statement.

While a signing statement can be used at the president's discretion, the statement is not to be considered more important than the original law itself.

Reference

> Wolley, J.T. (n.d.). *What is a signing statement. The American Presidency Project.* Retrieved from http://www.presidency.ucsb.edu/signingstatements.php#q1

Smear campaign A campaign effort developed by the opposition, aimed at calling into question, denigrating, or destroying the credibility or image of a candidate for public office.

Reference

> Darlington & Darlington, 2012.

Social media A form of electronic communication that includes web-based and mobile-based technologies which are used to turn communication into interactive dialogue between organizations, communities, and individuals. Andreas Kaplan and Michael Haenlein define social media as "a group of Internet-based applications that build on the ideological and technological foundations of the World Wide Web." Social networks allow the creation and exchange of user-generated content.

Reference

> Social media. (n.d.). In *Merriam-Webster online dictionary* (11th ed.). Retrieved from http://www.merriam-webster.com/dictionary/social%20media

Solicitor general An attorney who is charged with assisting the attorney general in arguing the position of the administration for cases that come in front of the U.S. Supreme Court.

Reference

> Solicitor General. (2006). In *Merriam-Webster's collegiate dictionary* (11th ed.). Springfield, MA: Merriam-Webster.

SOPA (H.R. 3261: Stop Online Piracy Act) A U.S. bill created in an effort to stop online piracy and expand the ability of law enforcement to fight the trafficking of online copy written material.

The bill was introduced by U.S. Representative Lamar Smith (R-TX) in 2012.

Reference

> H.R. 3261 Stop Online Piracy Act. (2011, Nov 16). *Statement of Maria A. Pallante, Register of Copyrights before the Committee on the Judiciary.* Retrieved from http://judiciary.house.gov/hearings/pdf/112%20HR%203261.pdf

Speaker of the House A member of the majority party in the House of Representatives is chosen as the Speaker and acts as leader of the House. This role combines the institutional role of presiding officer and administrative head of the House, the partisan role of leader of the majority party in the House, and the representative role of an elected member of the House. The Speaker of the House is second in line to succeed the president, after the vice president.

Reference

> United States House of Representatives. (2012). Speakers of the House. *House History.* Retrieved from http://artandhistory.house.gov/house_history/speakers.aspx

Did you know...

Appointed secretary of labor in 1939 by President Franklin D. Roosevelt, Frances Perkins was the first woman to serve in a presidential cabinet. She retained this office until 1945. Center for American Women and Politics: http://www.cawp.rutgers.edu/fast_facts/resources/Didyouknow.php#pres

Sponsor A congressional member who puts forth or authors a bill that is to be presented to the congressional body.

Stump speech A political speech, or series of speeches, given by a candidate for political office, that typically lays out the main platform positions of the candidate and his or her party. Oftentimes, this speech also serves to present a contrast between a given candidate and his opponent.

References

Darlington & Darlington, 2012.
Stump speech. (n.d.). In *Dictionary.com*. Retrieved from http://dictionary.reference.com/browse/stump+speech?qsrc=2446

Supermajority Most issues in the Senate are decided by a simple majority vote: one-half-plus-one of the members voting, assuming the presence of a quorum. However, the Senate has procedures that require either a two-thirds or a three-fifths vote. The super-majority requirements include the following: Invoke Cloture, Suspend the Rules, Postpone Treaty Consideration Indefinitely, Make a Bill a Special Order, The Senate, and Waive the Congressional Budget Act of 1974.

Reference

Olesk, W. (2010, April 12). *Super-majority votes in the Senate*. Congressional Research Service. U.S. Senate. Retrieved from http://www.senate.gov/CRSReports/crs-publish.cfm?pid=%26*2%3C4Q%3CG2%0A

Super PAC A political action committee that is allowed to raise and spend unlimited amounts of money from corporations, unions, individuals, and associations. They advocate for the election or defeat of candidates for federal office by purchasing television, radio, and print advertisements and other media.

Super PACs have no limitations on who can contribute or how much they contribute. They can raise as much money from corporations, unions, and associations as they want, and can spend unlimited amounts on advocating for the election or defeat of the candidates of their choice.

Super PACs are prohibited from working in conjunction with the candidates they're supporting.

Reference

SuperPAC. (n.d.). In *MacMillan online dictionary*. Retrieved from
http://www.macmillandictionary.com/open-dictionary/entries/superPAC.htm

Did you know...

The first woman to serve in the U.S. Senate was Rebecca Latimer Felton (D-GA).
She was appointed in 1922 and served for one day.
Center for American Women and Politics: http://www.cawp.rutgers.edu/fast_
facts/resources/Didyouknow.php#pres

Super Tuesday The second Tuesday in March, in a presidential election year,
on which a series of primary and caucus contests are held. This election day
is oftentimes considered one of the most reliable indicators for predicting the
eventual winner of the primary contest, which then leads to a general election.

Reference

Super-Tuesday. (n.d.). In *Longman dictionary of contemporary English*. Retrieved from
http://www.ldoceonline.com/dictionary/Super-Tuesday

Swift boat A term that originated during the 2004 presidential election in
reference to then candidate Senator John Kerry. The term, coined by the PAC,
Swift Boat Veterans for Truth, was meant to call into question the military
service of Senator John Kerry. The term swift boat refers to the type of boat
Senator John Kerry served on in Vietnam. A swift boat is a type of U.S. navy
patrol craft popular during the Vietnam War.

Reference

Annenberg Public Policy Center of the University of Pennsylvania. (2004, August
22). *Republican-funded group attacks Kerry's war record*. Retrieved from http://
www.factcheck.org/republican-funded_group_attacks_kerrys_war_record.html

Swing state A state that is considered to be relatively contestable among
the candidates in a political race or on a particular issue. In the U.S. electoral
system, these states are often referred to as "purple" states, due to its
classification as neither a "blue" or "red" state. Candidates for political office

tend to campaign more in these contested states, in an effort to swing the vote in their favor.

Reference

Swing state. (n.d.). In *Oxford dictionaries online*. Retrieved from http://oxforddictionaries.com/definition/swing%2Bstate

> *Did you know...*
>
> Some of the words added to the Merriam-Webster Dictionary in recent years include: crowdsourcing, m-commerce, Tweet, Social-network, fist-bump, helicopter-parent, bromance, Americana, duathalon, boomerang child, and cougar.
> Merriam-Webster Online: http://www.merriam-webster.com/info/newwords11.htm

T

Tax loophole A term which refers to particularly ambiguous or ill-defined tax policy which allows for maneuvering and manipulation on the part of those who aim to garner advantages by evading the policy.

Reference

Investopedia. (n.d.). *Loophole*. Retrieved from http://www.investopedia.com/terms/l/loophole.asp#axzz1wYVxyDiL

Tea Party An American political movement which originated in 2009 in response to recession, government-funded bailouts, and the fiscal irresponsibility members felt the U.S. government perpetuated. The movement is closely associated with an ideology that espouses fiscal responsibility, budget deficit reduction, and tax reform. While the movement has come to include positions regarding immigration, Second Amendment rights, and national health care policy, it still remains primarily a movement concerned with fiscal conservatism.

The movement received its name as a reference to the Boston Tea Party of 1773.

In the 2010 mid-term elections, the movement was able to help elect a number of national and state officials, who carried the Tea Party designation, to office.

Reference

Tea Party Patriots. (n.d.). About Us. Retrieved from http://www.teapartypatriots.org/

Term limits A policy that limits the number of terms a given elected official can serve in a particular capacity. This policy is often used to deter elected officials from dedicating a significant amount of resources, time, and effort to the reelection process, and it is believed that this system affords voters more choices in the electoral process. Some argue, however, that term limits actually limit a voter's choices, by preventing elected officials, who may be the best person for the position, to run for reelection.

Reference

Economic Definition of Term Limits Defined. (n.d.). *Economic glossary.* Retrieved from http://glossary.econguru.com/economic-term/term+limits

Terrorism There is no single, universally accepted definition of terrorism. Terrorism is defined in the Code of Federal Regulations as the unlawful use of force and violence against persons or property to intimidate or coerce a government, the civilian population, or any segment thereof, in furtherance of political or social objectives.

Reference

The Federal Bureau of Investigation. (2012). *Terrorism 2002-2005.* Retrieved from http://www.fbi.gov/stats-services/publications/terrorism-2002-2005

Third party A political party that is not one of the two dominant parties in any given electoral system. In the United States, specifically, the Democratic and Republican parties constitute the two main political parties within the electoral system. Third parties have included, but are not limited to, the Green Party, Libertarian Party, and Independent Party.

Reference

Third Party. (n.d.). In *Merriam-Webster online dictionary* (11th ed.). Retrieved from http://www.merriam-webster.com/dictionary/third%20party

Tweet A message, no more than 140 characters in length, that is sent out over the Internet via Twitter. Users of this social network can send messages to their followers, as well as receive messages from those they follow.

Reference

Twitter. (2012). About. Retrieved from http://twitter.com/about

Twitter© An Internet-based social network which allows users to post comments instantly. The comments are limited to 140 characters, and are linked to the users' account username. Each user can follow other users and other users can choose to follow them, as well. Politicians and celebrities, alike, have used this social networking engine to inform their followers and post political and personal commentary since its inception in 2006. While its first use was not for the purpose of sending out personal messages, it has since come to be used by people in almost every country in the world.

Reference

Twitter. (2012). About. Retrieved from http://twitter.com/about

V

Voting age population (VAP) The portion of a population that is, by virtue of their age, eligible to vote. This portion of the population may be excluded from voting by other factors; however, they are of appropriate age.

Reference

McDonald, M. (2010). *Voter turnout.* Frequently Asked Questions. Retrieved from http://elections.gmu.edu/FAQ.html

Voting eligible population (VEP) The portion of a population that is both of age to vote and eligible to engage in the franchise. If a person within a population, for example, has reached the age at which she can legally cast a ballot at the polls, but is excluded for another reason, not related to her age, she would not be considered part of the VEP. Some of these exclusionary factors could include, but are not limited to, immigration status or status as a felon.

Reference

> McDonald, M. (2010). *Voter turnout*. Frequently Asked Questions. Retrieved from http://elections.gmu.edu/FAQ.html

Wag the dog A colloquial term used to describe a political issue that is framed by interested parties in such a way that the deleterious effects of a poor political choice become a more salient issue than the original decision or action that caused it. Attention is diverted from the more important concern, and is then centered on the lesser concern of the two.

Reference

> De La Cruz, J. (2012, May 2). *Idiom: Wag the dog*. Retrieved from http://www.usingenglish.com/reference/idioms/wag+the+dog.html

War on terror A term coined by the George W. Bush administration to describe the policies the administration undertook during the aftermath of the events of September 11, 2001. These policies informed the way in which the United States dealt with certain elements in the Middle East, in an effort to curb terrorism in the region.

Reference

> War on Terrorism. (n.d.). In *The free online dictionary: Legal dictionary*. Retrieved from http://legal-dictionary.thefreedictionary.com/War+on+Terrorism

Wedge issue A term used to describe a political issue that is, or can be, used to further separate political party platforms, opposing positions on various issues, and to create greater contrast between political opponents.

Reference

McGowan, L. (n.d.). *Driving voters apart: Can a wedge issue be used to win an election.* Retrieved from http://www.thepresidency.org/storage/documents/Calkins/McGowan.pdf

Winner-take-all An electoral system that gives the total number of delegates from a particular state to one candidate when the candidate receives 50% plus one vote, in a political race. This system is an alternative to a system that affords candidates delegates based on the proportion of the vote they receive.

Reference

Killian, E.A. (n.d.). *U.S. political glossary.* Retrieved from http://www.killian.com/earl/glossary.html#winnertakeall

Weapon of mass destruction (WMD) A weapon with the capacity to inflict death and destruction on such a massive scale and so indiscriminately that its very presence in the hands of a hostile power can be considered a grievous threat. Modern weapons of mass destruction are nuclear, biological, or chemical.

The term weapons of mass destruction has been in currency since at least 1937, when it was used to describe massed formations of bomber aircraft.

The term gained contemporary significance following the attacks of September 11, 2001, and the subsequent invasion of Iraq. Saddam Hussein, then president of Iraq, was accused of harboring WMDs.

Reference

Weapon of Mass Destruction (WMD). (2012). In *Encyclopædia Britannica.* Retrieved from http://www.britannica.com/EBchecked/topic/917314/weapon-of-mass-destruction-WMD

About the Authors

Patricia St. E. Darlington

Dr. Darlington teaches courses in intercultural communication, ethnicity and communication, minorities and the media, and leadership and communication. Her research is focused on the study of women, power, and ethnicity and the exploration of cultural identities in the United States. Recent publications include *Cultural Minority Representation in the Media: A Historic View of Television's Underserved* (2011).

Rolda L. Darlington

Rolda L. Darlington is a former middle school teacher who earned her master's degree in political science and teaching at Florida Atlantic University. She is currently pursuing her doctorate in political science, with an emphasis in American politics and government, at the University of Florida.